WHAT WENT WRONG IN OHIO

WHAT WENT WRONG IN OHIO

The Conyers Report on the 2004 Presidential Election

Introduction by Gore Vidal

Edited by Anita Miller

ACADEMY
CHICAGO

This edition © 2005 by
Academy Chicago Publishers
363 West Erie Street
Chicago, Illinois 60610
www.academychicago.com

Introduction © 2005 Gore Vidal

Printed in the U.S.A.

ISBN 0-89733-535-X

Contents

INTRODUCTION

ONE OF THE MOST useful—currently *the* most useful—members of the House of Representatives is John Conyers, a Michigan Democrat who, in his capacity as ranking minority member of the House Judiciary Committee, led eleven Democratic Congressmen and their staffers into the heart of the American heartland, the Western Reserve—specifically, into the not-so-red state of Ohio, once known as "the mother of presidents."

Conyers had come to answer the essential question that the minority of Americans who care deeply about our republic have been asking since November, 2004: *"What Went Wrong in Ohio?"* He is too modest to note the difficulties he must have undergone even to assemble this team in the face of the triumphalist Republican Congressional majority—not to mention the unlikely heir, George W. Bush, whose original selection by the Supreme Court brought forth many reports on what went wrong in Florida in 2000. That led to an apology from Associate Justice John Paul Stevens for the behavior of the five-to-four majority of the Court in the matter of *Bush v. Gore*, which gave us loser Bush and his undeclared wars in Afghanistan and Iraq, as well as the greatest deficits in our history—to say nothing of an administration that eschews truth much as Count Dracula fled cloves of garlic, while fleeing also all accountability for the murder and torture of captive men (between 70% to 80% chosen at random is the Pentagon's estimate), earning us the hatred of a billion Moslems and the disgust of what is called the civilized world.

Before the late election, there was much discussion about how the unsuccessful war in Iraq would play with the voters. Could a Democrat win? Should it be Dean or Kerry? Dean, using the internet and a modicum of passion, raised more money than Democratic candidates are used to seeing; he also tapped into that deep mind-your-own-business attitude—which is a constant American characteristic, until the propagandists start exploiting the media in order to convince a majority of some terrifying untruth that will get them to go to war. The Bush Administration did not invent these tricks, but they certainly perfected them: *weapons of mass destruction poised at our blameless shores* was a lot more vivid than the 1916 slogan that re-elected Woodrow Wilson, another war-bound president: "He kept us out of war."

Asked to predict who would win in '04, I said that Bush would lose again, but I was confident that in the four years between 2000 and 2004, creative propaganda and the fixing of election officials might very well be so perfected as to ensure an official victory for Mr. Bush. As Representative Conyers' status report shows in great detail, the swing state of Ohio was carefully set up to deliver an apparent victory for Bush even though Kerry appears to have been not only the popular winner but also the valedictorian that-never-was of the Electoral College.

I urge would-be reformers of our politics, as well as of such anachronisms as the Electoral College, to read this valuable guide on how to steal an election, once you have in place the supervisor of the state's electoral process: in this case Ohio's Secretary of State Kenneth Blackwell, who orchestrated this famous victory for those who hate the democracy (a permanent but passionate minority). The Report states categorically, "With regards to our factual findings, in brief, we find that there were massive and unprecedented voter irregularities and anomalies in Ohio. In many cases these irregularities were caused by intentional misconduct and illegal behavior, much of it involving Secretary of State Kenneth Blackwell, the co-chair of the Bush-Cheney campaign in

Ohio." The same scenario redux as in Florida in 2000 when Katherine Harris, the then-Florida Chair for Bush-Cheney, was also Secretary of State. Lesson? Always plan ahead for at least four more years.

Even though it was well known that Ohio had a considerable number of first-time voters, "the deliberate misallocation of voting machines," thanks to Blackwell and his gang, "led to unprecedented long lines that disenfranchised scores, if not hundreds of thousands, of predominately minority and Democratic voters . . ."

For the last few years, many of us have been warning about the electronic voting machines, first publicized on the internet by the journalist Bev Harris—for which she was much reviled by the officers of such companies as Diebold, Sequoia, ES & S and Triad. This latter "voting computer company . . . has essentially admitted that it engaged in a course of behavior during the recount in numerous counties to provide 'cheat sheets' to those counting the ballots. The 'cheat sheets' informed election officials how many votes they should find for each candidate, and how many over and under votes they should calculate to match the machines' counts. In that way, they could avoid doing a full county-wide hand count mandated by state law."

Yet despite all this man power and money power, exit polls showed that Kerry would win Ohio. So, what happened?

I have told more than enough of this mystery story so thoroughly investigated by John Conyers and his eleven Congressional colleagues and their staffers. Not only were the crimes against the democracy investigated, but the Report comes up with quite a number of ways to set things right.

Needless to say, this Report was ignored when the Electoral College produced its unexamined tally of the votes state by state. Needless to say, no joint committee of the two Houses of Congress was convened to consider the various crimes committed and to find ways and means to avoid their repetition in 2008, should we be allowed to hold an election once we have unilaterally, yet again, engaged in a war—this time with Iran.

Anyway, thanks to Conyers, the writing is now high up there on the wall for us all to see clearly; "Mene, Mene, Tekel, Upharsin." Students of the Good Book will know what these words of God meant to Nebuchadnezzer and his friends in old Babylon.

GORE VIDAL
APRIL, 2005

EXECUTIVE SUMMARY

REPRESENTATIVE JOHN CONYERS, JR., the Ranking Democrat on the House Judiciary Committee, asked the Democratic staff to conduct an investigation into irregularities reported in the Ohio presidential election and to prepare a Status Report on that before the Joint Meeting of Congress scheduled for January 6, 2005, to receive and consider the votes of the electoral college for president. The following report includes a brief chronology of the events; provides detailed findings (including factual findings and legal analysis); describes various recommendations for acting on this report going forward; and summarizes the relevant background law.

We have found numerous serious election irregularities in the Ohio presidential election, which resulted in a significant disenfranchisement of voters. Cumulatively, these irregularities, which affected hundreds of thousands of votes and voters in Ohio, raise grave doubts about whether it can be said that the Ohio electors selected on December 13, 2004, were chosen in a manner conforming to Ohio law, let alone Federal requirements and constitutional standards.

This report, therefore, makes three recommendations:

(1) Consistent with the requirements of the United States Constitution concerning the counting of electoral votes by Congress and Federal law implementing these requirements, there are ample grounds for challenging the electors from the State of Ohio.

(2) Congress should engage in further hearings into the widespread irregularities reported in Ohio. We believe the problems are serious enough to warrant the appointment of a joint Select Committee of the House and Senate to investigate and report back to the Members.

(3) Congress needs to enact election reform to restore our people's trust in our democracy. These changes should include putting in place more specific Federal protections for Federal elections, particularly in the areas of audit capability for electronic voting machines and casting and counting of provisional ballots, as well as other needed changes to Federal and State election laws.

As to our factual finding: in brief, we find that there were massive and unprecedented voter irregularities and anomalies in Ohio. In many cases these irregularities were caused by intentional misconduct and illegal behavior, much of it involving Secretary of State J. Kenneth Blackwell, the co-chair of the Bush-Cheney campaign in Ohio.

I. In the run-up to Election Day, the following actions by Mr. Blackwell, the Republican Party and election officials, disenfranchised hundreds of thousands of Ohio citizens, predominantly Minority and Democratic voters:

A. The misallocation of voting machines led to unprecedented long lines that disenfranchised scores, if not hundreds of thousands, of predominantly Minority and Democratic voters. The *Washington Post* reported that in Franklin County, "27 of the 30 wards with the most machines per registered voter showed majorities for Bush. At the other end of the spectrum, six of the seven wards with the fewest machines delivered large margins for Kerry."[1] Among other things, the conscious failure to provide sufficient voting machinery violates the Ohio Revised Code, which requires the Boards of Elections to "provide adequate facilities at each polling place for conducting the election."

B. **Mr. Blackwell's decision to restrict provisional ballots resulted in the disenfranchisement of tens, if not hundreds, of thousands of voters, again predominantly Minority and Democratic voters.** Mr. Blackwell's decision departed from past Ohio law on provisional ballots; there is no evidence that a broader construction would have led to any significant disruption at the polling places. It did not do so in other states.

C. **Mr. Blackwell's widely reviled decision to reject voter registration applications based on paper weight may have resulted in thousands of new voters not being registered in time for the 2004 election.**

D. **The Ohio Republican Party's decision to engage in pre-election "caging" tactics, selectively targeting 35,000 predominantly minority voters for intimidation, had a negative impact on voter turnout.** The Third Circuit Court found these activities to be illegal and in direct violation of consent decrees barring the Republican Party from targeting minority voters for poll challenges.

E. **The Ohio Republican Party's decision to utilize thousands of partisan challengers concentrated in minority and Democratic areas probably disenfranchised** tens of thousands of legal voters, who were not only intimidated, but became discouraged by the long lines. Shockingly, these disruptions were publicly predicted and acknowledged by Republican officials: Mark Weaver, a lawyer for the Ohio Republican Party, admitted the challenges "can't help but create chaos, longer lines and frustration."

F. Mr. Blackwell's decision to prevent voters who requested absentee ballots, but did not receive them on a timely basis, from being able to receive provisional ballots probably disenfranchised thousands, if not tens of thousands, of voters, particularly seniors. A Federal court found Mr. Blackwell's order to be illegal and in violation of HAVA (Help America Vote Act).

II. On Election Day, there were numerous unexplained anomalies and irregularities involving hundreds of thousands of votes that have yet to be accounted for:

A. There were widespread instances of intimidation and misinformation in violation of the Voting Rights Act, the Civil Rights Act of 1968, Equal Protection, Due Process and the Ohio right to vote. Mr. Blackwell's apparent failure to institute a single investigation into these many serious allegations represents a violation of his statutory duty under Ohio law to investigate election irregularities.

B. We learned of improper purging and other registration errors by election officials that probably disenfranchised tens of thousands of voters statewide. The Greater Cleveland Voter Registration Coalition projects that in Cuyahoga County alone, over 10,000

Ohio citizens lost their right to vote as a result of official registration errors.

C. **There were 93,000 spoiled ballots where no vote was cast for president, the vast majority of which have yet to be inspected.** The problem was particularly acute in two precincts in Montgomery County which had an under-vote rate of over 25% each—accounting for nearly 6,000 voters who stood in line to vote, but supposedly declined to vote for president.

D. **There were numerous significant, unexplained irregularities in other counties throughout the state:**

1. In Mahoning county, at least twenty-five electronic machines transferred an unknown number of Kerry votes to the Bush column;

2. Warren County locked out public observers from vote counting, citing an FBI warning about a potential terrorist threat. But the FBI states that it issued no such warning;

3. The voting records of Perry county show significantly more votes than voters in some precincts, significantly fewer ballots than voters in other precincts, and voters casting more than one ballot;

4. In Butler county, a downballot and underfunded Democratic State Supreme Court candidate implausibly received more votes than the best-funded Democratic Presidential candidate in history;

5. In Cuyahoga county, poll-worker error may have led to little-known third party candidates receiving twenty times more votes than such candidates had ever received in otherwise reliably Democratic-leaning areas;

6. In Miami county, voter turnout was an improbable and highly suspect 98.55 percent, and after 100 percent of the precincts were reported, an additional 19,000 extra votes were recorded for President Bush.

III. In the post-election period, we learned of numerous irregularities in tallying provisional ballots and conducting and completing the recount that disenfranchised thousands of voters and called the entire recount procedure into question. (As of the date of this report, the recount is still not complete.):

A. Mr. Blackwell's failure to articulate clear and consistent standards for the counting of provisional ballots resulted in the loss of thousands of predominately Minority votes. In Cuyahoga County alone, the lack of guidance and the ultimate narrow and arbitrary review standards significantly contributed to the fact that 8,099 out of 24,472 provisional ballots were ruled invalid, the highest proportion in the state.

B. Mr. Blackwell's failure to issue specific standards for the recount contributed to a lack of uniformity in violation of both the Due Process clause and the Equal Protection clauses. We found innumerable irregularities in the recount in violation of Ohio law, including:

1. counties which did not randomly select the precinct samples;

2. counties which did not conduct a full hand count after the 3% hand-and-machine counts did not match;

3. counties which allowed irregular marking of ballots and failed to secure and store ballots and machinery; and

4. counties which prevented witnesses for candidates from observing the various aspects of the recount.

C. **The voting computer company Triad has essentially admitted that it engaged in a course of behavior during the recount in numerous counties to provide "cheat sheets" to those counting the ballots.** The cheat sheets informed election officials how many votes they should find for each candidate, and how many over- and under-votes they should calculate to match the machine count. In that way, they could avoid doing a full county-wide hand recount mandated by State law.

Chronology of Events

The Lead-Up to the 2004 Ohio Presidential Election in Ohio

In the days leading up to Election Day 2004, a consensus appeared to have emerged among observers that Ohio would be one of the battleground states that would decide who would be elected the forty-fourth President of the United States.[2] Both the Democratic and Republican Presidential campaigns, as well as outside groups, had spent considerable time and resources to win the state, but the day before the election, the Democratic candidate, Senator John Kerry, appeared to have the edge.[3] The Democratic Party also had vastly out-performed its Republican counterparts in registering voters in this key state.[4]

Election Day

Numerous irregularities were reported throughout Ohio. In predominately Democratic and African American areas in particular, the voting process was chaotic, taxing and ultimately fruitless for many. The suspect repeated challenges of voter eligibility, and the lack of an adequate number of voting machines in these areas, worked in concert to slow voting to a crawl, with voting lines lasting as long as ten hours.[5] Voters reported bizarre "glitches" in voting machines, where votes for Senator Kerry were registered as votes for the President.[6] The counting process was similarly chaotic and suspect.

THE AFTERMATH

On November 5, after receiving preliminary reports of election irregularities in the 2004 General Election, Congressman John Conyers, Jr., the Ranking Member of the House Judiciary Committee, and fourteen Members of Congress, wrote to the Government Accountability Office (GAO) to request an investigation of these irregularities.[7]

On November 22, at the request of the GAO, the Democratic staff of the House Judiciary Committee met with GAO officials. In this meeting, GAO officials advised that, on its own authority, the GAO was prepared to move forward with a wide-ranging analysis of systemic problems in the 2004 elections. GAO officials also advised Judiciary staff that they would be unable to examine each and every specific election complaint, but would look at some of these complaints as exemplars of broader deficiencies.

At the same time, the offices of Democratic staff and Democratic Judiciary Committee Members were deluged with e-mails and complaints about the election. Close to 100,000 such complaints were received, and are still being processed. As of this writing, the Judiciary Democratic office alone is receiving approximately 4,000 such e-mails a day. More than half of these complaints were from one state: Ohio. The Election Protection Coalition has testified that it received more complaints on Election Day concerning irregularities in Ohio than irregularities in any other state.[8]

On December 2, 2004, Members of the Judiciary Committee wrote to Ohio Secretary of State Kenneth Blackwell that these complaints appear collectively to constitute a troubled portrait of a one-two punch that may well have altered and suppressed votes, particularly Minority and Democratic votes. The Members posed thirty-six questions to Secretary Blackwell about a combination of official actions and corresponding actions by non-official persons, who, whether in concert or separately, worked hand-in-glove to depress the vote among constituencies deemed by Republican campaign officials to be disadvantageous to them.

Through his spokesman, Secretary Blackwell assured the public and the press that he would be happy "to fill in the blanks" for the Committee and asserted that many questions were easily answered. In fact, Secretary Blackwell belatedly replied to the Committee's letter with a refusal to answer **any** of the thirty-six questions. Ranking Member Conyers wrote back to Mr. Blackwell the same day requesting that he remain true to his promise to answer the questions. Congressman Conyers has yet to receive a reply.

At the same time, officials from the Green Party and the Libertarian Party have been investigating allegations of voter disenfranchisement in Ohio and other states. Eventually, the presidential candidates for those parties, David Cobb and Michael Badnarik, respectively, filed requests to all eighty-eight Ohio counties for recounts. However, it appears their efforts too are being stonewalled and thwarted by non-standard and highly selective recounts, unnecessary delays, and blatant deviations from long-accepted Ohio law and procedure. Recently, Senator Kerry, a party to the recount action, joined the Green Party and Libertarian Party in requesting immediate action to halt these irregularities and potential fraud in the recount. The recount is still pending before the Federal court, and valid votes have yet to be counted.

In addition, a challenge has been filed to the Ohio results asserting, to a level of sworn proof beyond a reasonable doubt, that Senator Kerry, not President Bush, was the actual victor of the presidential race in Ohio. Kenneth Blackwell is adamantly refusing to answer any questions under oath about election irregularities or results. He is apparently counting upon Congress accepting the votes of the electors and, as an immediate consequence, the Ohio Supreme Court dismissing the citizens' election contest.

Committee Members and other interested Members have gone to substantial lengths to ascertain the facts of this matter. The investigation by Congressman Conyers and the Democratic staff of the House Judiciary Committee into the irregularities reported in the Ohio presidential election has also included the following efforts:

On November 5, 2004, Representatives Conyers, Nadler, and Wexler wrote to GAO Comptroller David M. Walker, requesting an investigation of the voting machines and technologies used in the 2004 election.

On November 8, 2004, Representatives Conyers, Nadler, Wexler, Scott, Watt, and Holt wrote to GAO Comptroller Walker requesting that additional concerns surrounding the voting machines and technologies used in the 2004 election be investigated.

On November 15, 2004, Representatives Lee, Filner, Olver, and Meeks joined in the request for a GAO investigation.

On November 29, 2004, Representatives Weiner, Schakowsky, Farr, Sanders, and Cummings joined in the request for a GAO investigation.

On December 2-3, 2004, Congressman Conyers and other Judiciary Democratic Members wrote to Ohio

Secretary of State J. Kenneth Blackwell concerning Ohio election irregularities.

On December 3, 2004, Representative Woolsey joined in the request for a GAO investigation.

On December 3, 2004, Congressman Conyers wrote to Warren Mitofsky of Mitofsky International, requesting the release of exit-poll raw data from the 2004 presidential election since such data may evidence instances of voting irregularities.

On December 8, 2004, Congressman Conyers hosted a forum in Washington, D.C., on voting irregularities in Ohio.

On December 13, 2004, Congressman Conyers hosted a second forum in Columbus, Ohio, on voting irregularities in Ohio.

On December 13, 2004, Congressman Conyers and other Members wrote to Ohio Governor Bob Taft, Speaker of Ohio State House Larry Householder, and President of Ohio State Senate Doug White, requesting a delay of the meeting of Ohio's presidential electors.

On December 14, 2004, Congressman Conyers wrote to Ohio Secretary of State J. Kenneth Blackwell about the Secretary's refusal to cooperate with the Judiciary Democratic Members' investigation of election irregularities in Ohio.

On December 15, 2004, Congressman Conyers wrote to FBI Special Agent in Charge Kevin R. Brock and Hocking County, Ohio, Prosecutor Larry Beal, requesting an investigation into alleged Ohio election problems.

On December 21, 2004, Congressman Conyers wrote to Ohio candidates requesting that they report any incidents of irregularities or deviations from accepted law or practices during the recount in Ohio.

On December 21, 2004, Congressman Conyers wrote to several major media outlets requesting the exit poll raw data from the 2004 presidential election.

On December 22, 2004, Congressman Conyers wrote to Triad GSI President Brett Rapp and Triad GSI Ohio Field Representative Michael Barbian, Jr., concerning the voting machine company's involvement in the Presidential election, the Ohio recount, and allegations that Triad intentionally or negligently acted to prevent validly cast ballots in the Presidential election from being counted.

On December 23, 2004, as a follow-up letter to the December 22 letter, Congressman Conyers wrote to Triad President Rapp and Ohio Field Representative Barbian upon learning that Triad had remote access to tabulating computers controlled by the Board of Elections.

On January 3, 2005, Federal and Ohio State lawmakers joined Reverend Jesse Jackson in Columbus, Ohio for a rally calling attention to the need for national election reform and to the January 6th Joint Session of Congress where election results [are] certified.

Citizen groups have played a substantial role in acquiring relevant information. The Citizens Alliance for Secure Elections in Ohio has held organized hearings that have provided valuable leads for this report. We have been contacted by thousands of concerned citizens: they want a full and fair count of all of the votes and they wish to have confidence in the electoral system: they find both of these to be sorely lacking in this election. Many have investigated these matters themselves and have made considerable sacrifices to do so.

The events surrounding the presidential election in Ohio must be viewed in two important contexts. First, there is the 2000 election debacle in Florida. In that election, advocates for a full and fair count were asked to "move on" after Vice President Al Gore conceded the election to Governor George W. Bush. Months later, it was found that a full and fair count would have resulted in Gore, not Bush, being elected the Forty-third President of the United States.[9] Subsequent investigations also uncovered rampant disenfranchisement in Florida, particularly of African American voters.[10]

Second, as events have unfolded in Ohio, telling events have taken place within the United States, in the State of Washington, and across the globe in Ukraine. In Washington State, the Republican gubernatorial candidate, Dino Rossi, declared victory after a partial recount;[11] it was later found—after a full and fair recount—that the Democratic candidate, Christine Gregoire, was the victor.[12] While national and state Republican leaders in Ohio have derided attempts to ascertain the Ohio Presidential Election result and resolve the questions described herein, Mr Rossi, after the Washington recount, has asked for a re-vote in the State of Washington, saying it is needed for the election to be "legitimate."[13]

In Ukraine, after the apparent defeat of the opposition leader Viktor Yushchenko in that nation's presidential election, allegations of fraud and public protests caused a new election to be held, which Yushchenko won by a significant margin.[14] In fact, in the first, seemingly flawed election, Yushchenko appeared to lose by three percentage points.[15] However, he won by eight percentage points in the subsequent revote.[16] United States officials called the original vote rife with "fraud and abuse," largely relying on anecdotal evidence and deviations between exit polls and reported results.[17]

A simple lesson may be drawn from these two contexts: elections are imperfect. They are subject to manipulation and mistakes. It is therefore critical that elections be investigated and audited to assure the accuracy of results. As Senator Kerry's attorney recently noted, only with uniformity in the procedures for such an investigation and audit "can the integrity of the entire electoral process and the election of Bush-Cheney warrant the public trust."[18]

Regardless of the outcome of the election—and that outcome cannot be certain as long as legitimate questions remain, and valid ballots are being counted—it is imperative that we examine any and all factors that may have led to voting irregularities and any failure of votes to be properly counted.

Detailed Findings

I. Pre-Election

A. MACHINE ALLOCATIONS—WHY WERE THERE SUCH LONG LINES IN DEMOCRATIC-LEANING AREAS, BUT NOT REPUBLICAN-LEANING AREAS?

FACTS

One of the critical reforms of HAVA (Help America Vote Act) was federal funding for states to acquire new and updated voting machines, and to fairly allocate the machines. Under HAVA, the Election Assistance Commission (EAC) provides payments to states to help them meet the uniform and nondiscriminatory election technology and administration requirements in Title III of the law.[19] In 2004, the EAC processed a payment of $32,562,331 for fiscal year 2003 and $58,430,186 for fiscal year 2004, for a total of $90,992,517.[20] There is no information publicly available describing what, if any, Ohio HAVA funds were used and for what purpose those funds were used. Nor do we know how such funds were allocated within the state of Ohio and amongst counties.

There was a wide discrepancy between the availability of voting machines in heavily Minority, Democratic and urban

17

areas as compared to heavily Republican, suburban and exurban areas. Even on Election Day, urban areas were hard pressed to receive the critical machines to respond to the ever-lengthening lines. According to a *Washington Post* investigation, "in Columbus, Cincinnati and Toledo, and on college campuses, election officials allocated far too few voting machines to busy precincts, with the result that voters stood on line as long as ten hours—many leaving without voting."[21] Moreover, the Election Protection Coalition testified that more than half of the complaints about long lines they received "came from Columbus and Cleveland where a huge proportion of the state's Democratic voters live."[22]

Based upon various sources—including complaints, sworn testimony, and communications with Ohio election officials—we have identified credible concerns regarding the allocation of machines on Election Day.

1. FRANKLIN COUNTY

A *New York Times* investigation revealed that Franklin County election officials reduced the number of electronic voting machines assigned to downtown precincts and added them to the suburbs. "They used a formula based not on the number of registered voters, but on past turnout in each precinct and on the number of so-called active voters—a smaller universe. . . . In the Columbus area, the result was that suburban precincts that supported Mr. Bush tended to have more machines per registered voter than center city precincts that supported Mr. Kerry."[23]

The *Washington Post* found that in voter-rich Franklin County, which encompasses the state capital of Columbus, election officials decided to make do with 2,866 machines, even though their analysis showed that the county needed 5,000 machines.[24]

The Franklin County Board of Elections reported that 81 voting machines were **never** placed on Election Day, and Board Director Matt Damschroder admitted that another 77 machines malfunctioned on Election Day.[25] However, a county purchasing official who was on line with Ward Moving and Storage Company, documented only 2,741 voting machines delivered through the November 2 Election Day,[26] while Franklin County's records reveal that they had 2,866 "machines available" on Election Day.[27] This would mean that the even larger number of at least 125 machines remained unused on Election Day. Mr. Damschroder misinformed a Federal court on Election Day when he testified the county had no additional voting machines; this testimony was in connection with a Voting Rights Act lawsuit brought by the state Democratic Party alleging that Minority precincts were intentionally deprived of machines.[28]

After the election, the *Washington Post* reported that in Franklin County, "27 of the 30 wards with the most machines per registered voter showed majorities for Bush. At the other end of the spectrum, six of the seven wards with the fewest machines delivered large margins for Kerry."[29]

At seven of the eight polling places in Franklin County, a heavily populated urban community, there were only three voting machines per location; but there had been five machines at these locations during the 2004 primary.[30] According to the presiding judge at one polling site located at the Columbus Model Neighborhood facility at 1393 E. Broad St., there had been five machines during the 2004 primary.[31] Moreover, at Douglas Elementary School, there had been four machines during the spring primary.[32]

We have received additional information, based on e-mails and other transmissions, of hardship caused by the misallocation of machines, with waits of four to five hours or more being the order of the day. For example, we have learned of four-hour waits at Precincts 35B and C in Columbus; seven hour waits for one voting machine per 1000 voters, where the adjacent precinct had one station for 184 voters.[33] Additionally, it appears that in a number of locations, polling places were moved from large locations, like gyms, where voters could comfortably wait inside to vote, to smaller locations where voters were required to wait in the rain.[34]

Dr. Bob Fitrakis testified before the House Judiciary panel that the Franklin County Board of Elections Chair, Bill Anthony, said that a truckload of seventy-five voting machines were held back on Election Day while people waited five to six hours to vote.[35]

Over 102,000 new voters were registered in Franklin County. A majority of them were African Americans. "And so," said State Senator Ray Miller, "only logic would say we need more machines, particularly in the black community."[36]

Rev. William Moss testified that there were "unprecedented long lines" and noted that Secretary of State Blackwell did not provide sufficient numbers of voting machines to accommodate the augmented electorate in Columbus.[37]

2. KNOX COUNTY

At Kenyon College, a surge of late registrations promised a record vote. Nevertheless, Knox County officials allocated two machines, as in past elections.[38] Voter Matthew Segal, a student at Kenyon College, testified before the House Judiciary panel about conditions that amounted to voter disenfranchisement in Gambier, Ohio.[39] The Gambier polling place had two machines for a population of 1,300 people, though nearby counties had one machine for every 100 people.[40] Mr

Segal noted that voters were "compelled to stand outside in the rain, then go into a hot gymnasium through crowded, narrow hallways, making voting extremely uncomfortable."[41] According to his testimony, "many voters became overheated and hungry" and had to leave the long lines to eat. "One girl actually fainted and was forced to leave the line," he said. "Many others suffered headaches due to claustrophobic conditions and noise."[42]

In contrast, at nearby Mt. Vernon Nazarene University, which is considered more Republican-leaning, there were ample voting machines and no lines.[43]

OTHER

The NAACP testified that approximately "thirty precincts did not have curbside voting machines for seniors and disabled voters."[44]

One entire polling place in Cuyahoga County had to "shut down" at 9:25 a.m. on Election Day because there were no working machines.[45]

We received an affidavit from Rhonda J. Frazier, a former employee of Secretary Blackwell, describing several irregularities concerning the use of HAVA money and the acquisition of election machinery by the state. She states that Secretary Blackwell's office failed to comply with the requirements of the voting reform grant that required all voting machines in Ohio to be inventoried and tagged for security reasons. Ms. Frazier asserts also that she "was routinely told to violate the bidded contracts to order supplies from other companies for all 17 Secretary of State offices throughout the State which were cheaper vendors, leaving a cash surplus differential in the budget" and that, when she inquired about where the money differential was going, she was essentially told that this was not her concern and that she should not ask where that money went.[46]

Secretary of State Blackwell has refused to answer any of the questions concerning these matters posed to him on December 2, 2004, by Ranking Member Conyers and eleven other Members of the Judiciary Committee.[47]

ANALYSIS

Through intent or negligence, massive errors that led to long lines were made in the distribution and allocations of voting machines. **The *Washington Post* reports that in Columbus alone, the misallocation of machines reduced the number of voters by up to 15,000 votes.[48] Given what we have learned in our hearings, this is probably a conservative estimate, and statewide, the shortage of machines could have resulted in the loss of hundreds of thousands of votes.** The vast majority of this lost vote—caused by lengthy lines in the midst of adverse weather—was concentrated in urban, Minority and Democratic-leaning areas. As a result, this misallocation appears to be one of the pivotal factors concerning the vote and the outcome in the entire election in Ohio.

On its face, the misallocation, shorting, and failure of timely deliverance of working machines would appear to violate a number of legal requirements.

Firstly, it would seem to constitute a violation of the Voting Rights Act and the Constitutional safeguards of Equal Protection and Due Process, particularly given the racial disparities involved. Denying voters the means to vote in a reasonable and fair manner is no different from preventing them from voting outright.

Secondly, the failure to provide enough voting machinery violates both Ohio's Constitution, that provides all eligible adults the right to vote, and the Ohio Revised Code which requires the Boards of Elections to provide "for each

precinct a polling place and provide adequate facilities at each polling place for conducting the election."[49] Further, "the board shall provide a sufficient number of screened or curtained voting compartments to which electors may retire and conveniently mark their ballots."[50]

These conclusions concerning Ohio legal violations are supported by several precedents, as well as by common sense:

> The U.S. District Court for the Southern District of Ohio found so serious a threat to the voting right that it took the highly unorthodox step of ordering that those individuals waiting in line for longer than two hours receive paper ballots or some other mechanism to enable them to vote.[51]
>
> There is specific precedence for consideration of these actions as legal violation: under Ohio law in 1956, the courts were forced to intervene to enforce the then-applicable requirement of one machine per 100 voters.[52] The court was highly critical of the previous practice of requiring only one machine for 800 voters or two for 1,400.[53] Nearly fifty years later, we are unfortunately back to the antiquated practice of effectively disenfranchising those who are unable to spend an entire day trying to vote.
>
> Evidence suggests that the Board of Elections' misallocation of machines went beyond urban/suburban discrepancies to specifically target Democratic areas. In particular, within the less urban county of Knox, the more Democratic-leaning precincts near Kenyon College were massively shorted; the more Republican-leaning precincts near Mt. Vernon Nazarene University were not shorted at all.

Thirdly, it appears that a series of more localized legal violations have not been investigated. These include Mr.

Damschroder's contradictory statements concerning the number and availability of machines on Election Day in Franklin County, which raise the possibility of perjury. The affidavit submitted by Rhonda Frazier would also appear to demonstrate a *prima facie* violation of the Help America Vote Act.

Fourthly, Secretary of State Blackwell's failure to initiate any investigation into this pivotal irregularity (which perhaps borders on fraud), despite his clear statutory duty to do so under Ohio Revised Code section 3501.05, represents a clear violation of Ohio law. The Secretary of State's most important obligation under the Ohio Constitution is to protect the right of every Ohio citizen who is eligible to vote and to investigate any and all irregularities concerning that right. Mr. Blackwell's failure to obey Ohio law on this point constitutes a clear instance of abrogation of Ohio election law.

B. CUTTING BACK ON THE RIGHT TO PROVISIONAL BALLOTS

FACTS

On September 17, 2004, in a decision that Ohio Governor Bob Taft believed could affect over 100,000 voters,[54] Secretary Blackwell issued a directive restricting the ability of voters to use provisional ballots. The Election Protection Coalition testified that the narrow Provisional Ballot directive led to thousands of ballots from validly registered voters being thrown out because election officials with limited resources never told many of the voters in their jurisdictions where to cast their ballots on Election Day.[55] While the Help America Vote Act provides that voters whose names do not appear on poll books are to sign affidavits certifying that they are in the correct jurisdiction and are to be given provisional ballots, Secretary Blackwell considerably narrowed the definition of "jurisdiction" to mean "precinct."[56] Alleging that allowing voters to use provisional ballots outside their own precincts would be "a recipe for Election Day chaos," Secretary Blackwell required these ballots to be cast in the actual precincts of voters; otherwise, they would be discarded entirely.[57] Mr. Blackwell's rationalization appears to have ignored the fact that in prior elections, Ohio was able to grant far broader rights to provisional ballots, and that in other states permitting voters to cast these ballots from anywhere within their county, no "chaos" ensued.

The Sandusky County Democratic Party filed a Federal lawsuit to overturn Secretary Blackwell's restrictive order.[58] The plaintiff's basis for the suit was that the order was discriminatory because lower-income people were more likely to move and thus appear at the wrong precinct.[59] Furthermore, the order would have disenfranchised first-time voters, many of whom would not know where to go to vote.[60]

In his rulings in favor of the plaintiffs, U.S. District Judge James Carr held that the blame lay squarely on Secretary Blackwell.[61] The court was forced to issue two rulings ordering Secretary Blackwell to issue HAVA-compliant directives. Secretary Blackwell abided by neither judgment and instead proceeded with directives that would disenfranchise Ohio voters.

With respect to the speed of the case, the court noted that its urgency was the result of Secretary Blackwell failing to issue provisional voting guidelines for almost two years after the enactment of HAVA:

The exigencies requiring the relief being ordered herein are due to the failure of the defendant to fulfill his duty not only to this Court, as its injunction directed him to do, but more importantly, to his fail-

ure to do his duty as Secretary of State to ensure
that the election laws are upheld and enforced. . . .
The primary cause of the exigency is the defendant's
failure to have issued Directive 2004-33 relating to
provisional voting for nearly twenty-three months
after HAVA's enactment. . . . Blackwell has never
explained why he waited so long to do anything to
bring Ohio's provisional election procedures into line
with federal law.[62]

The court then turned its attention to the substance of
Secretary Blackwell's original and amended directives. In
these directives, "Blackwell described not a single provision of federal law generally, much less HAVA in particular.
. . . By failing to discuss HAVA, on the one hand, and describing only outmoded, no longer applicable procedures
on the other, Blackwell . . . left Ohio's election officials more
confused than they would have been if the directive had not
[been] issued."[63] In addition, because the amended directive did not clearly state that persons who might not be
eligible to vote must be informed of their right to vote pro-
visionally, the court held that "Blackwell's proposed directive would disenfranchise all such individuals."[64] The court
believed that, by seeming to deprive voters and county election officials of valuable information regarding HAVA and
provisional ballots, "Blackwell apparently seeks to accomplish the same result in Ohio in 2004 that occurred in Florida
in 2000."[65] Ultimately, the court was forced to require the
Secretary, within a tight deadline, to issue specific guidelines on provisional ballots.[66]

Instead of complying with this Federal court order, Secretary Blackwell entirely disregarded the ruling and questioned the motives of the judge. He referred to Judge Carr
as "a liberal judge . . . who wants to be co-secretary of

state."[67] At a speech before the Loveland Area Chamber of Commerce in Clermont County, Secretary Blackwell compared himself to Mohandas Gandhi, Martin Luther King, and the Apostle Paul, on the grounds that he would rather go to jail—as they did—than issue an order he believed was illegal.[68] He also claimed his office could not speak with Judge Carr about the case because the judge was in Florida; Blackwell later admitted he did not mean the judge was actually in Florida.[69] A journalist reported seeing Judge Carr in his chambers the day the ruling was issued.[70] Secretary Blackwell appealed the judge's decision to the Sixth Circuit Court of Appeals, which overturned the lower court decision and authorized Mr. Blackwell's more restrictive legal interpretation.

While Mr. Blackwell cited an October 12 resolution by the Election Assistance Commission as authority for his decision, EAC Chairman DeForest Soaries asked Mr. Blackwell in writing not to say that the resolution endorsed the Blackwell order.[71] Chairman Soaries further stated that Secretary Blackwell was the only secretary of state who actually misread the EAC's ruling.[72] The EAC did not "agree that a person in the wrong precinct shouldn't be given a provisional ballot. . . . The purpose of provisional ballots is to not turn anyone away from the polls. . . . We want as many votes to count as possible."[73]

Many of Ohio's County Boards of Elections also disagreed with Mr. Blackwell's interpretation of the law and with his motivations.[74] Franklin County Board Chairman William Anthony stated, "For him to come out with that decision so close to Election Day . . . I'm suspect of his motivations."[75] The Director of the Franklin County Board also disagreed with Mr. Blackwell and asserted that in its precincts, voters who insist they are in the correct precinct, sign affidavits and

submit provisional ballots.[76] Cuyahoga County directed
people to the right precincts, but accepted provisional ballots
from anyone who insisted on voting.[77] Cuyahoga County
Board Chairman Bob Bennett, who also chairs the Ohio Republican Party, issued a statement saying the Board would
not deny ballots to voters who wanted them:

> The Cuyahoga County Board of Elections will not
> turn voters away. . . . We are simply trying to avoid
> confrontation at the ballot box over the validity of
> each ballot. Those decisions will be made by the
> board of elections according to state law.[78]

In response, Mr. Blackwell's spokesperson threatened
such election officials with removal from their positions.[79]

In Hamilton County, election officials implemented Mr.
Blackwell's directive and refused to count provisional ballots cast at the correct polling place, but at the wrong **table**
in that polling place.[80] Some polling places contained multiple precincts that were located at different tables.[81] As a
result, 1,110 provisional ballots were deemed invalid because people voted in the wrong precinct. In about 40% of
these cases, voters were at the correct polling places, which
contained multiple precincts, but workers directed them to
the wrong table.[82] In other areas, precinct workers refused
to give any voter a provisional ballot.[83] Also, in at least one
precinct, election judges told voters that they could validly
cast their ballot in any precinct; this led to any number of
disqualified provisional ballots.[84] Similarly, in Stark County,
the Election Board rejected provisional ballots cast at the
right polling place, but in the wrong precinct. In earlier elections, a vote cast in Stark County in the wrong precinct at
the proper polling location was counted.[85]

Secretary of State Blackwell has refused to answer any of the questions in connection with these matters posed to him on December 2, 2004 by Ranking Member Conyers and eleven other Members of the Judiciary Committee.[86]

ANALYSIS

Mr. Blackwell's decision to restrict the use of provisional ballots is one of the most critical in the election and could well have resulted in the disenfranchisement of tens of thousands of voters. In a single polling place in Hamilton County, denying provisional ballots if a voter showed up at the wrong precinct, cost more than 1,100 votes.

Although Mr. Blackwell's narrow interpretation was ultimately upheld by the Sixth Circuit, this was not until after a lower court found:

> The Proposed Directive fails in many details to comply with HAVA by not instructing Ohio's election workers about their duties under HAVA. Among the crucial, but omitted, details are: the mandatory obligation to inform voters of the right to vote provisionally and the duty to provide provisional ballots to all persons covered by the statute, and not just to persons whose names are not on the rolls.[87]

In our judgment, Mr. Blackwell's restrictive interpretation violates the spirit, if not the letter, of HAVA. The decision seems particularly unjust given that Ohio had not experienced any notable difficulties giving provisional ballots on a broader basis in past elections, and other states which adopted broader constructions did not report the chaos and confusion that Mr. Blackwell claimed as the rationale for his decision.

C. CUTTING BACK ON THE RIGHT OF CITIZENS TO REGISTER TO VOTE

FACTS

On September 7, 2004, Secretary Blackwell issued a directive to County Boards of Elections mandating rejection of voter registration forms based on their paper weight. Specifically, he instructed the boards to reject voter registration forms not "printed on white, uncoated paper of not less than 80 lb. text weight."[88] Then the counties were instructed to follow a confusing procedure, declaring the voter registration forms invalid which were not printed on 80 lb. paper.[89] Mr. Blackwell's issuance of this directive less than one month before Ohio's voter registration deadline, resulted in confusion and chaos among the counties:

> The Lake County Board of Elections Director, Jan Clair, a Republican, stated that the weight order would "create more confusion than the paper's worth. . . . It's the weight of the vote I'm concerned about on Nov. 2—that's the important thing."[90]
>
> The Mahoning County Board of Elections Director, Michael Sciortino, said mailing high weight registration paper to voters was not a priority and might confuse voters.[91]
>
> The Cuyahoga County Board of Elections Director, Michael Vu, said his board would rather not comply with the weight order and asked state lawmakers to address it.[92]
>
> Secretary Blackwell gave permission for the board to accept registration forms printed on newsprint in the *Cleveland Plain Dealer*.[93] As Director Vu pointed out, his office does not "have a micrometer at each desk to check the weight of the paper."[94]

Other counties such as Madison County followed Mr. Blackwell's ruling, sending letters and new forms to voters.[95]

The Franklin County Board of Elections was unlikely to comply with the weight directive, largely because it does not keep track of the weight of such forms.[96]

The Lorain County Board of Elections accepted voter registrations on any weight of paper.[97]

The Montgomery County Board of Elections said the paper weight order was frustrating their ability to process registrations.[98] They attempted to comply by mailing a new form to potential voters who submitted forms on paper of proscribed weight, but a processing backlog of 4,000 forms prevented them from sending new forms by the October 4 deadline, so some voters could have been disenfranchised.[99] Steve Harsman, the Deputy Director of the Board, says, "There is just no reason to use 80-pound paper."[100]

Finally, Secretary Blackwell did not follow his own order. An Ohio lawyer, John Stopa, noted that voter registration forms obtained at Blackwell's office were printed on 60-pound paper.[101] An election board official stated he obtained 70-pound weight forms from Blackwell's office.[102]

After several weeks of pressure from voting rights advocates like the League of Women Voters of Ohio and People for the American Way,[103] Secretary Blackwell reversed his directive on September 28, 2004.[104] Even his new order, however, was not drafted clearly enough. He did not withdraw the first directive, and the *New York Times* found the second directive to be "worded so inartfully that it could create confusion."[105] As a matter of fact, the Delaware County Board of Elections posted a notice on its website stating it could not accept its own Voter Registration Forms and directed voters to request a new one by calling a telephone number.[106]

Secretary of State Blackwell has refused to answer any of the questions concerning these matters posed to him on December 2, 2004, by Ranking Member Conyers and eleven other Members of the Judiciary Committee.[107]

ANALYSIS

Secretary Blackwell's directive to reject registration applications based on paper weight, even though eventually rescinded, undoubtedly had a negative impact on registration figures. During the period the directive was in place, the probable result was that an untold number of voters were not registered in time for the 2004 election. In addition, the directive was withdrawn in a confusing manner. For example, the directive continued to be posted on the Ohio Secretary of State's website,[108] and at least one county, Delaware County, continued to post the directive on its website.

Mr. Blackwell's initial directive appears to be inconsistent with the National Voter Registration Act, which put safeguards in place to *ease* voter registration, not to impede it. There is perhaps no more certain indication of the disenfranchisement bias Secretary of State Blackwell brought to his job than this controversial ruling, which was widely reviled even by Republicans.

D. TARGETING NEW MINORITY VOTER REGISTRANTS—"CAGING"

FACTS

The Ohio Republican Party attempted to engage in "caging": it sent registered letters to newly registered voters in

Minority and urban areas, and then sought to challenge 35,000 individuals who refused to sign for the letters or whose mail otherwise came back as undeliverable. This number includes voters who were homeless, serving abroad, or simply did not want to sign for mail from the Republican Party. Mark Weaver, an attorney for the Ohio Republican Party, acknowledged that the Party used this technique.[109] During a hearing before the Summit County Board of Elections, a challenger admitted that she was not able to substantiate her claim that the voters she challenged were out of compliance with Ohio's election law:[110]

Barbara Miller, Republican Challenger: That was my impression that these items that I signed were for people whose mail had been undeliverable for several times, and that they did not live at the residence.

Mr. Russell Pry, Member, Summit County Board of Elections: Did you personally send any mail to Ms. Herrold?

Ms. Miller: No, I did not.

Mr. Pry: Have you seen any mail that was returned to Ms. Herrold?

Ms. Miller: No, I have not.

Mr. Pry: Do you have any personal knowledge as we stand here today that Ms. Herrold does not live at the address at 238 30th Street Northwest?

Ms. Miller: Only that which was my impression; that their mail had not been able to be delivered.

Mr. Pry: And who gave you that impression?

Ms. Miller: Attorney Jim Simon.

Mr. Pry: And what did—

Ms. Miller: He's an officer of the party.

Mr. Pry: An officer of which party?

Ms. Miller: Republican party.

Mr. Pry: Where did you complete this challenge form at?

Ms. Miller: My home.

Mr. Pry: What did Mr. Simon tell you with respect to Ms. Herrold's residence?

Ms. Miller: That the mail had come back undeliverable several times from that residence.

Mr. Pry: And you never saw the returned mail?

Ms. Miller: No, I did not.

Mr. Pry: Now, you've indicated that you signed this based on some personal knowledge.

Mr. Joseph F. Hutchinson, Jr. Summit County Board of Elections: No!

Mr. Alex R. Arshinkoff, Summit County Board of Elections: Reason to believe. It says, "I have reason to believe." It says it on the form.

Mr. Jones: It says, "I hereby declare under penalty of election falsification, that the statements above are true as I verily believe."

Mr. Arshinkoff: It says here, "I have reason to believe."

Mr. Hutchinson: It says what it says.

Mr. Arshinkoff: You want her indicted, get her indicted.

Mr. Pry: That may be where it goes next.

* * *

Among other things, the Republican Party arranged for the Sandusky County sheriff to visit the residences of 67 voters with wrong or non-existent addresses.[111]

The caging tactics were so problematic that a Federal District Court in New Jersey and a panel of the Third Cir-

cuit found that the Republican Party was egregiously in violation of the 1982 and 1987 decrees that barred the party
from targeting Minority voters for challenges at the polls.[112]
They found sufficient evidence that the Ohio Republican
Party and the RNC conspired to be "disruptive" in minor-
ity-majority districts and enjoined the party from using the
list.[113] The Third Circuit granted a hearing en banc and therefore stayed the order and vacated the opinion.[114]

The U.S. District Court for the Southern District of Ohio
found that these same activities violated the Due Process clause
of the Constitution.[115] Most importantly, notice of the Re-
publican-intended challenge and subsequent hearing was sent
to the 35,000 voters far too late to be of any use to the
challengee.[116] In fact, the notice was sent so late that many
did not receive it before the election at all, and the court found
that ineffective notice must have been the intent:

> The Defendants' intended timing and manner of
> sending notice is not reasonably calculated to ap-
> prise Plaintiff Voters of the hearing regarding the
> challenge to their registrations, nor to give them the
> opportunity to present their objections, as demon-
> strated by the individual situations of Plaintiffs Miller
> and Haddix . . . it seems that Defendants intend to
> send the notice to an address which has already been
> demonstrated to be faulty.[117]

The court also found that the challenge statute in general was not narrowly tailored enough to justify the "severe" burden on voters.[118] While the state's interest in preventing fraudulent voting was compelling, there were other
ways to accomplish that without allowing partisan groups
to arbitrarily challenge voters.[119]

ANALYSIS

Although the "caging" tactics targeting 35,000 new voters by the Ohio Republican Party were eventually struck down, it is probable that they had a negative impact on the inclination of minorities to vote; although, it is difficult to develop a specific estimate.

The caging tactics were clearly both discriminatory and illegal. All three district court cases ruled in favor of the plaintiffs, finding the challenges to be politically and racially charged. One court stated: "This Court recognizes that the right to vote is one of our most fundamental rights. Potential voter intimidation would severely burden the right to vote. Therefore, the character and magnitude of Plaintiffs' asserted injury is substantial."[120] The court went on to note that the right to vote is paramount to any interest in challenging other people: ". . . Plaintiff's right to cast votes on election day is a fundamental right. The challengers, however, do not have a fundamental right to challenge other voters.[121] These decisions correctly overturned these caging and challenging activities because **they violated the right to equal protection, due process, and Ohioans' fundamental right to vote.**

Ralph Neas, President of the People for the American Way Foundation, emphasized the seriousness of these tactics when he testified that "35,000 people . . . were threatened with being challenged. That's not the spirit of democracy; that's the spirit of suppression. [The Republican Party] did everything to minimize the vote in the urban areas and to engage in voter suppression, and I hope the hearings really emphasize this. I think that prosecution is something that should be considered with respect to what happened in Ohio."[122]

E. TARGETING MINORITY AND URBAN VOTERS FOR LEGAL CHALLENGES

FACTS

The Ohio Republican Party, which Secretary Blackwell helped lead as Chair of the Bush-Cheney campaign in Ohio, engaged in a massive campaign to challenge Minority voters at the polls.[123] The Republican Party lined up poll challengers for 30 of Ohio's 88 counties, and the vast majority were focused in Minority and urban areas.[124] In addition to intimidating Minority voters, this scheme led to increased delays and longer waits in voting lines in these areas. This was a particularly damaging outcome on a day of severe weather in Ohio. A Federal court looking at these issues concluded that **"if challenges are made with any frequency, the resultant distraction and delay could give rise to chaos and a level of voter frustration that would turn qualified electors away from the polls."**[125]

Three separate courts issued opinions expressing serious concerns with Ohio's voter challenge processes. At the state level, Judge John O'Donnell of the Cuyahoga County Common Pleas Court, found that Secretary Blackwell exceeded his authority in issuing a directive that allowed each political party to have multiple challengers at each polling place.[126] While the Democratic Party registered only one challenger per polling place, the Republican Party had registered one challenger for each *precinct* (there are multiple precincts in many polling places).[127] Judge O'Donnell found the directive to be "unlawful, arbitrary, unreasonable and unconscionable, coming **four days after the deadline** for partisan challengers to register with their county boards of elections."[128] An attorney with the Ohio Attorney General's office, Jeffrey Hastings, admitted to Judge O'Donnell that Secretary Blackwell had changed his mind—at first limiting challengers to one per polling place and then, after the October 22 challenger registration deadline, allowing multiple challengers.[129]

Two Federal District Court judges also found the challenge procedure to be problematic and tantamount to voter disenfranchisement.[130] In one lawsuit, the plaintiffs were Donald and Marian Spencer, an elderly African American couple who alleged that the challenge statute harkened back to Jim Crow disenfranchisement. In her opinion rejecting the GOP challenger system, U.S. District Court Judge Susan Dlott wrote that "there exists an enormous risk of chaos, delay, intimidation and pandemonium inside the polls and in the lines out the door."[131] In the other district court case, *Summit County Democratic Central and Executive Committee, et. al. v. Blackwell*, Judge John R. Adams noted the risk that "the integrity of the election may be irreparably harmed."[132] "If challenges are made with any frequency," he wrote, "the resultant distraction and delay could give rise to chaos and a level of voter frustration that would turn qualified electors away from the polls."[133]

Judge Dlott also noted the racial disparity inherent in challenges, citing that only 14% of new voters in white areas would face challenges, while up to 97% of new voters in black areas would face them.[134] The Chair of the Hamilton County Board of Elections, Timothy Burke, was an official defendant in the lawsuit, but testified that the use of the challenges was unprecedented.[135] Chairman Burke testified also that the Republican Party had planned for challengers at 251 of Hamilton County's 1013 precincts; 250 of the challenged precincts have significant black populations.[136]

Both Federal courts blocking the use of challengers highlighted the fact that challengers were not needed because Ohio law already safeguarded elections from voter fraud by the use of election judges.[137] In particular, Ohio law mandates that four election judges staff each polling place and provides that the presiding judge of each group can make decisions on voter qualifications.[138]

Although Secretary Blackwell reversed his position and issued a statement on October 29, 2004, excluding challengers from polling places, his reversed position was undercut when Jim Petro, Ohio Attorney General, argued in favor of the challenges taking place and said the secretary's new statement was unlawful.[139] Seeing the irony in these conflicting opinions, Judge Dlott asked, "How can the average election official or inexperienced challenger be expected to understand the challenge process if the two top election officials cannot?"[140]

These two lower court rulings did not stand. The Sixth Circuit Court of Appeals reversed the two lower court opinions on a 2-1 vote.[141] The Supreme Court of the United States denied the applications to vacate the 6th Circuit's stays of the lower court rulings.[142] While troubled about the "undoubtedly serious" accusation of voter intimidation, Justice John Paul Stevens said the full Court could not consider the case because there was insufficient time to properly review the filings and submissions.[143]

ANALYSIS

The decision by the Ohio Republican Party to utilize thousands of partisan challengers in the voting booths undoubtedly had an intimidating and negative impact on Minority voters. While it is difficult to estimate how many voters were disenfranchised by the challenger program, given the adverse weather conditions and the lack of trained pollworkers, the disruptions caused by challengers could easily have reduced Minority turnout by tens of thousands of voters, if not more. It is noteworthy that these disruptions were predicted by Republican officials:

> **Mark Weaver, a lawyer for the Ohio Republican Party, acknowledged, "[The challenges] won't be resolved until [Election Day], when all of these people are trying to vote. It can't help but create chaos, longer lines and frustration."[144] He reiterated that "[challengers at the polls] were "bound to slow things down. This will lead to long lines."[145]**

While the program of challenging voters was ultimately upheld after a series of back and forth decisions, clearly this is an issue which recalls the "Jim Crow" era. U.S. District Court Judge John R. Adams wrote in his Summit County opinion:

> In light of these extraordinary circumstances, and the contentious nature of the imminent election, the Court cannot and must not turn a blind eye to the substantial likelihood that significant harm will result not only to voters, but also to the voting process itself, if appointed challengers are permitted at the polls on November 2. . . . The presence of appointed challengers at the polls could significantly impede the electoral process, and infringe on the rights of qualified voters."[146]

As a result, the Ohio challenger system deserves reconsideration by the legislature or further judicial appeal.

F. DENYING ABSENTEE VOTERS WHO NEVER GOT THEIR BALLOTS THE RIGHT TO A PROVISIONAL BALLOT

FACTS

Secretary Blackwell also issued a ruling preventing the issuance of provisional ballots for voters who requested absentee ballots, even if they failed to receive the absentee ballots by the official deadline or did not receive them at all.[147] Despite the fact that these errors occurred due to the actions on the part of the Ohio government and were not the fault of the voters, Secretary Blackwell determined they should not receive provisional ballots at the polls.

A lawsuit filed by Sara White, a college student who never received her absentee ballot and was denied a provisional one, led to a ruling that other voters in the same circumstances must be issued provisional ballots.[148] The court ordered Lucas County to start providing provisional ballots, and directed Secretary Blackwell to advise all Boards of Elections of this ruling within thirty minutes.[149] The legal ruling overturning Mr. Blackwell's restrictive ruling on absentee ballots came late in the afternoon, and as a result, many voters intending to vote that day were prevented from doing so.

ANALYSIS

Mr. Blackwell's decision to prevent those voters—who requested absentee ballots, but did not receive them on a timely basis—from being able to vote, also probably disenfranchised many voters, particularly seniors who were turned away from the polls before the decision was known.

The Federal court found that Mr. Blackwell's decision clearly violated HAVA: "HAVA is clear; that all those who appear at a polling place and assert their eligibility to vote irrespective of the fact that their eligibility may be subject to question by the people at the polling place or by the Board of Elections, shall be issued a provisional ballot."[150] **In addition, this restrictive directive also probably constituted violations of Article 5, Section 1, of the Ohio Constitution, granting every Ohio citizen the right to vote if he or she is otherwise qualified.**

G. DENYING ACCESS TO THE NEWS MEDIA

FACTS

Secretary Blackwell also sought to prevent the news media and exit-poll takers from coming within 100 feet of polling places.[151] This would have been the first time in thirty years in which reporters were prevented from monitoring polls.[152] Media organizations challenged the barrier, leading to a ruling from the U.S. Court of Appeals for the Sixth Circuit striking down Secretary Blackwell's decision.[153] In its opinion, the court noted that "democracies die behind closed doors"[154] and found that the District Court's ruling had "interpreted and applied the statute overly broadly in such a way that the statute would be violative of the first amendment."

ANALYSIS

Mr. Blackwell's decision to prevent news media and exit polls from interviewing Ohio citizens after they voted constitutes a clear violation of the First Amendment's guarantee that state conduct shall not abridge "freedom . . . of the press."[155] His decision also probably violated Ohio's own Constitution that provides: "Every citizen may freely speak, write, and publish his sentiments on all subjects, being responsible for the abuse of the right; and no law shall be passed to restrain or abridge the liberty of speech, or of the press."[156] His decision does not appear to have had any negative impact on the vote, but potentially made it more difficult for the media to uncover voting irregularities, discrepancies, and disenfranchisement.

II. ELECTION DAY

A. COUNTY-SPECIFIC ISSUES

1. Warren County—Counting in Secret Because of a Terrorist Threat?

FACTS

On election night, Warren County, a traditional Republican stronghold, locked down its administration building and barred reporters from observing the counting.[157] When that decision was questioned, County officials claimed they were responding to a terrorist threat that ranked a "10" on a scale of 1 to 10, and that this information was received from an FBI agent.[158] Despite repeated requests, County officials have declined to name that agent, and the FBI has stated that it had no information about a terror threat in Warren County.[159]

Warren County officials have given conflicting accounts of when the decision was made to lock down the building.[160] The County Commissioner has stated that the decision to lock down the building was made during an October 28 closed-door meeting, but e-mailed memos—dated October 25 and 26—indicate that preparations for the lockdown were already underway.[161] Statements also describe how ballots were left unguarded and unprotected in a warehouse on Election Day, and were hastily moved after county officials received complaints.[162]

It is important to view the lockdown in the context of the aberrant results in Warren County. An analyst who has received all the vote data for 2000 and 2004 by precinct in several Ohio counties, did a detailed analysis of the increase in votes for President Bush by precinct, and the Bush-Kerry margin in Warren County.[163] The analyst revealed that Warren County first did a lockdown to count the votes, then apparently did another lockdown to recount the votes later, resulting in an even greater Bush margin and very unusual new patterns.[164]

Moreover, in the 2000 presidential election, the Democratic presidential candidate, Al Gore, stopped running television commercials and pulled resources out of Ohio weeks before the election. He won 28% of the vote in Warren County.[165] In 2004, the Democratic presidential candidate, John Kerry, fiercely contested Ohio, and independent groups also put considerable resources into getting out the Democratic vote. Moreover, unlike in 2000, independent candidate Ralph Nader was not on the Ohio ballot in 2004. Yet the tallies show John Kerry receiving exactly the same percentage, 28%, in Warren County as Gore received in 2000.[166]

In support of his assertion that there was no wrongdoing in Warren County, Secretary Blackwell has mentioned Jeff Ruppert, a Democratic election observer in Warren County, who has said he observed nothing inappropriate at the County administration building. While we have no reason to doubt Mr. Ruppert's account of what he actually observed, a complete review of his statements shows there were a number of problems at the Warren County Administration Building. At the outset, Mr. Ruppert acknowledges that he was subject to the lockout and had to present identification even to be admitted to the building.[167] Once he gained admission, Mr. Ruppert said he did "have concerns over how provisional ballots were handled at polling places—which he said seemed to be inconsistent."[168] He also pointed to a number of areas he observed that were centers of activity: ballots being transferred from vehicles, precinct captains with ballots in elevators, and ballots being stored. But, clearly, it would have been impossible for Mr. Ruppert to observe all of these activities at the same time. Finally, considering that he left before the ballot count was completed,[169] it is inaccurate to state with certainty that there were no problems in Warren County.

Secretary of State Blackwell has refused to answer any of the questions concerning these matters posed to him by Ranking Member Conyers and eleven other Members of the Judiciary Committee on December 2, 2004.[170]

ANALYSIS

Given the total lack of explanation by Mr. Blackwell or Warren County officials, it is not implausible to assume that someone is hiding something. We do not know whether what happened is simply a miscommunication or the result of a confused situation in which an election official misunderstood an FBI directive. If that were the case, it would seem to be an easy matter to dispel the confusion. Given that no such explanation has been forthcoming and given the statistical anomalies in the Warren County results, it is impossible to rule out the possibility that some sort of manipulation of the tallies occurred on election night in the locked-down facility. The disclosure that the decision to lock down the facility the Thursday *before* the election, rather than on Election Day, would suggest the lockdown was a political decision and not a real security risk. If that was the case, it would be a violation of the Constitutional guarantees of Equal Protection and Due Process, the Voting Rights Act, and the Ohio right to

vote. We believe it is the statutory duty of the Secretary of
State to investigate irregularities of this nature.

2. Mahoning County—Innumerable Flipped Votes and Extra Votes

FACTS

We have received numerous reports of votes for Senator
Kerry transferred to votes for President Bush. Specifically,
the *Washington Post* reported that their investigation in
Youngstown revealed that twenty-five electronic machines
transferred an unknown number of Kerry votes to the Bush
column.[171] Jeanne White, a veteran voter and manager at
the *Buckeye Review,* an African American newspaper,
stepped into the booth, pushed the button for Kerry—and
watched her vote jump to the Bush column. "I saw what
happened; I started screaming, 'They're cheating again and
they're starting early!'"[172] The Election Protection Coalition
also confirmed these voting "glitches," noting that a voter
reported, "Every time I tried to vote for the Democratic
Party Presidential vote the machine went blank. I had to
keep trying, it took five times."[173]

The voting machine in Youngstown was afflicted by
what election officials called "calibration problems."[174]
Thomas McCabe, Deputy Director of the Mahoning County
Board of Elections, stated that the problem "happens every
election" and "[i]t's something we have to live with and we
can fix it."[175]

There is also information, still being investigated, that
in several precincts, there were more votes counted by machine than signatures in poll books (which includes absentee voters). This would mean that more people voted by
machine at a precinct than actually appeared at that loca-

tion. For example, in CMP 4C Precinct, there were 279 signatures and 280 machine votes. In BLV 1 Precinct, there were 396 signatures, but 398 machine votes. In AUS 12 Precinct, there were 372 signatures, but 376 machine votes. In POT 1 Precinct, there were 479 signatures, but 482 machine votes, and in YGN 6F Precinct, there were 270 signatures, but 273 machine votes. It would appear from these numbers that the machines counted more votes than voters.

Secretary of State Blackwell has refused to answer any of the questions concerning these matters posed to him by Ranking Member Conyers and eleven other Members of the Judiciary Committee on December 2, 2004.[176]

ANALYSIS

Evidence strongly suggests many individuals voting in Mahoning County for Senator Kerry had their votes recorded for President Bush. **Due to lack of cooperation from Secretary of State Blackwell, we have not been able to ascertain the number of votes that were impacted or whether the machines malfunctioned due to intentional manipulation or error.** This would help us determine if the Voting Rights Act was also violated. Ascertaining the precise cause as well as the culprit could help ensure that the error does not occur in the future. Secretary of State Blackwell's apparent failure to initiate any investigation into this serious computer error would seem inconsistent with his statutory duty to review these matters.

3. Butler County—The Strange Case of the Downballot Candidate Outperforming the Presidential Candidate

In Butler County, a Democratic candidate for State Supreme Court, C. Ellen Connally, received 59,532 votes.[177] In contrast, the Kerry-Edwards ticket received only 54,185 votes,

5,000 fewer than the State Supreme Court candidate.[178] In addition, the victorious Republican candidate for State Supreme Court received approximately 40,000 *fewer* votes than the Bush-Cheney ticket.[179] Further, Connally received 10,000 or more votes in excess of Kerry's total number of votes in five counties and 5,000 more votes than Kerry's total in ten others.[180]

According to media reports of Ohio judicial races, Republican judicial candidates were "awash in cash," with more than $1.4 million in campaign funding, as well as additional independent expenditures made by the Ohio Chamber of Commerce.[181]

Secretary of State Blackwell has refused to answer any of the questions concerning these matters posed to him by Ranking Member Conyers and eleven other Members of the Judiciary Committee on December 2, 2004.[182]

ANALYSIS

It appears implausible that 5,000 voters waited in line to cast votes for an underfunded Democratic Supreme Court candidate and then declined to cast a vote for the most well-funded Democratic Presidential campaign in history. We have been unable to find an answer to the question of how an underfunded Democratic State Supreme Court candidate could receive such a disproportionately large number of votes in Butler County over the Kerry-Edwards ticket. This raises the possibility that thousands of votes for Senator Kerry were lost, either through manipulation or mistake. The loss of these votes would probably violate constitutional protections of equal protection and due process; if manipulation is involved, that would also violate the Voting Rights Act and Ohio election law.[183] This anomaly calls for an investigation, which Mr. Blackwell has failed to initiate.

4. Cuyahoga County—Palm Beach County for Pat Buchanan-Redux?

FACTS

It has been well documented that a flawed Palm Beach County ballot design in the 2000 Florida presidential election may well have cost Al Gore thousands of votes by misrecording such votes as votes for Pat Buchanan.[184] A similar problem may well have occurred in Cleveland in 2004.

Precincts in Cleveland have reported an incredibly high number of votes for third-party candidates who have historically received only a handful of votes from these urban areas. For example, precinct 4F in the 4th Ward cast 290 votes for Kerry, 21 for Bush, and 215 for Constitution Party candidate Michael Peroutka.[185] In 2000, the same precinct cast fewer than eight votes for all third party candidates combined.[186] This pattern is found in at least ten precincts throughout Cleveland in 2004, awarding hundreds of unlikely votes to the third party candidate.[187] Notably, these precincts share more than a strong Democratic history; they share the use of a punch card ballot.[188] This problem was created by the combination of polling sites for multiple precincts, coupled with incorrect information provided by poll workers.

In Cuyahoga County, each precinct rotates candidate ballot position.[189] Therefore, each ballot must go into a machine calibrated for its own precinct so that the voter's intent will be counted.[190] In these anomalous precincts, ballots were fed into the wrong machine, switching Kerry votes into third party votes.[191] This was done on the advice of poll workers who told voters that they could insert their ballots into any open machine—and machines were not clearly marked indicating that they would work only for their designated precinct.[192]

Secretary of State Blackwell has refused to answer any of the questions concerning these matters posed to him by Ranking Member Conyers and eleven other Members of the Judiciary Committee on December 2, 2004.[193]

ANALYSIS

It appears that hundreds, if not thousands, of votes intended to be cast for Senator Kerry were recorded for a third-party candidate. At this point it is unclear whether these voting errors resulted from worker negligence and error or intentional manipulation. While Cuyahoga County election official Michael Vu said he would investigate,[194] there has been no further explanation about what will be done to remedy this situation, and Secretary of State Blackwell has refused to cooperate in our investigation or pursue his own inquiry. **In any event, those voters whose votes were not properly counted suffered a violation of their Constitutional right to Equal Protection and Due Process; if intentional manipulation is involved, this would also violate the Voting Rights Act and Ohio election law.**[195]

5. Franklin County (Gahana)—How does a computer give George W. Bush nearly 4,000 extra votes?

FACTS

On Election Day, a computerized voting machine in ward 1B in the Gahana precinct of Franklin County recorded a total of 4,258 votes for President Bush and 260 votes for Democratic challenger John Kerry.[196] However, there are only 800 registered voters in that Gahana precinct, and only 638 people cast votes at the New Life Church polling site.[197] It has since been discovered that a computer glitch resulted in the recording of 3,893 extra votes for President George

W. Bush[198]—the numbers were adjusted to show President Bush's actual vote count at 365 votes and Senator Kerry's at 260 votes.[199]

Secretary of State Blackwell has refused to answer any of the questions concerning these matters posed to him by Ranking Member Conyers and eleven other Members of the Judiciary Committee on December 2, 2004.[200]

ANALYSIS

At this point it is unclear whether the computer glitch was intentional or not, as we have received no cooperation from Secretary Blackwell or other authorities in resolving the question. In order to resolve this issue for future elections, it must be determined how it was initially discovered that such a computer glitch did occur and what procedures were employed to alert other counties upon the discovery of the malfunction. Further, a determination should be made as to whether we can be absolutely certain that this particular malfunction did not occur in other counties in Ohio during the 2004 Presidential election, and what actions have been taken to ensure that this type of malfunction does not happen in the future.

6. Miami County—Where did nearly 20,000 extra votes for George W. Bush come from?

FACTS

In Miami County, voter turnout was a highly suspect and improbable 98.55 percent.[201] With 100% of the precincts reporting on Wednesday, November 3, 2004, President Bush received 20,807 votes, or 65.80% of the vote, and Senator Kerry received 10,724 votes, or 33.92% of the vote.[202] Thus, Miami County reported a total of 31,620 voters. Inexplicably, nearly 19,000 new ballots were added after all precincts reported, boosting President Bush's vote count to 33,039, or 65.77%, while Senator Kerry's vote percentage stayed exactly the same to three-one-hundredths of a percentage point at 33.92 percent.[203] Roger Kearney of Rhombus Technologies, Ltd., the reporting company responsible for vote results of Miami County, stated that the problem was not with his reporting and that the additional 19,000 votes were added before 100% of the precincts were in.[204]

Secretary of State Blackwell has refused to answer any of the questions concerning these matters posed to him by Ranking Member Conyers and eleven other Members of the Judiciary Committee on December 2, 2004.[205]

ANALYSIS

Mr. Kearney's statement does not explain how the vote count could change for President Bush, but not for Senator Kerry, after 19,000 new votes were added to the roster. Thus, we are primarily concerned with identifying a valid explanation for the statistical anomaly that showed virtually identical ratios after the final 20-40% of the votes were counted. Specifically, we have received no explanation as to how the vote count in this particular county could have changed for President Bush, but not for Senator Kerry, after 19,000 new votes were added to the roster. **The vote results in Miami constitute yet another significant anomaly in the tens-of-thousands range without any explanation or investigation by Secretary of State Blackwell,** leading us to conclude that there is probably some vote error or vote manipulation. **This could constitute a violation of Constitutional guarantees of Equal Protection and Due Process and, if intentional, would probably violate the Voting Rights Act and Ohio election law.**[206]

7. Perry County—Discrepancy in Number of Votes and Voters

FACTS

The House Judiciary Committee Democratic staff has received information indicating discrepancies in vote tabulations in Perry County.* Similar discrepancies have been found in other counties: for example, in Trumbull County there are apparently more absentee votes than absentee voters, according to a recent study.[207] Another example: the sign-in book for the Reading S precinct indicates that approximately 360 voters cast ballots in that precinct;[208] in the same precinct, the sign-in book indicates that 33 absentee votes were cast.[209] In sum, this would appear to mean that fewer than 400 total votes were cast in that precinct. Yet, the precinct's official tallies indicate that 489 votes were cast.[210] In addition, some voters' names have two ballot stub numbers listed next to their entries, creating the appearance that voters were allowed to cast more than one ballot.[211]

In another precinct in Perry County, W Lexington G AB, 350 voters are registered according to the County's initial tallies.[212] Yet, 434 voters cast ballots.[213] As the tallies indicate, this would be an impossible 124% voter turnout.[214] The breakdown on election night was initially reported to be 174 votes for Bush and 246 votes for Kerry.[215] We are advised that the Perry County Board of Elections has since issued a correction, claiming that due to a computer error, some votes were counted twice.[216] We are advised that the new tallies state that only 224 people voted, and the tally is

---

* As originally published, this section contained allegations of absentee ballot irregularities in Trumbull County. Upon further investigation, we have confirmed that those allegations were based on incomplete data and cannot be supported.

90 votes for Bush and 127 votes for Kerry.[217] This would make it appear that virtually every ballot was counted twice, which seems improbable.

In Madison Township, Precinct AAS, a review of the poll books shows that 481 people signed in to vote on Election Day,[218] yet the Perry County Board of Elections is reporting that 493 votes were cast in that precinct,[219] a difference of 13 votes. The same discrepancy appears with respect to Monroe Township AAV. The poll books show that 384 people signed in on Election Day to vote,[220] while the Perry County Board of Elections reports that 393 votes were cast,[221] a difference of 9 votes.[222]

We have also received information that in at least three precincts, Pike West AAY, New Lexington I AB, and Redfield AAC, more signatures appear in the sign-in books than votes cast. This would indicate that votes may have been discarded.[223]

In Perry County, there appears to be an extraordinarily high level of 91% voter registration; yet, a substantial number of these voters have never voted and have no signature on file.[224] Of the voters that are registered in Perry County, an extraordinarily large number of voters are listed as having registered in 1977, a year in which there were no Federal elections.[225] Of these, an unusual number are listed as having registered on the exact same day: in total, 3,100 voters apparently registered in Perry County on November 8, 1977.[226]

In addition, according to a Democratic staff count of the poll books, there are approximately 751 registered voters in Madison Township AAS,[227] while the Perry County Board of Elections reports that there are 850 registered voters in that township.[228]

Secretary of State Blackwell has refused to answer any of the questions concerning these matters posed to him by

Ranking Member Conyers and eleven other Members of the Judiciary Committee on December 2, 2004.[229]

ANALYSIS

Clearly, there is an unexplained discrepancy between the actual vote tallies and the number of registered voters in various precincts, along with other statistical anomalies in the county. **Given the lack of any explanation to date, and an absence of willingness by Secretary Blackwell or any other authorities to explain or investigate these irregularities, it is not inconceivable that some sort of vote tampering has occurred. If so, that would probably constitute a denial of the Constitutional guarantees of Equal Protection and Due Process, the Voting Rights Act, and Ohio election law.**[230]

Republicans in the State of Washington are currently citing such "mystery voters" as evidence of fraud. The State Republican Chairman has commented, "People ask me what fraud would look like? It would look like this."[231]

B. MYRIAD OTHER PROBLEMS AND IRREGULARITIES

We learned about literally thousands upon thousands of additional irregularities in Ohio. As a matter of fact, the Election Protection Commission has testified that, to date, there have been over 3,300 incidents of voting irregularities entered for Ohio alone.[232] Following is a brief highlight of some of the more egregious irregularities of which we have learned during the course of our investigation.

1. Intimidation and Misinformation

FACTS

The NAACP testified that it received over 200 calls reporting incidents of suspected voter intimidation or unusual election-related activities, particularly intimidation by challengers of poll workers and voters. A caller reported that someone was going door to door telling people they were not registered to vote. A voter in Franklin County received information in the mail identified as being from the state telling him that he would have to vote by provisional ballot because he had moved; in fact, the voter had not moved and had lived at the address for ten to fifteen years. One polling place worker asked only African American voters for their address. A new voter was told that there were vote challengers at her precinct. When she was voting, she became confused by the punch cards, but was afraid to ask poll workers for help for fear that she would be challenged. Demands by vote challengers that voters provide ID, caused many people to leave without voting. This egregious behavior should be curtailed by the state.[233]

In Franklin County, a worker at the Holiday Inn observed a team of twenty-five people who called themselves the "Texas Strike Force," using payphones to make intimidating calls to likely voters, targeting people who had recently been in prison. These "Texas Strike Force" members paid their own way to Ohio, but their hotel accommodations were paid for by the Ohio Republican Party, whose headquarters is across the street. The hotel worker heard one caller threaten a likely voter that he would be reported to the FBI and sent back to jail if he voted. Another hotel worker called and reported this to the police, who came, but did nothing.[234]

Phone calls were placed, falsely informing voters that their polling places had changed.[235]

The *Cleveland Plain Dealer* found that several Lake County residents received an official-looking letter on Board of Elections letterhead informing them that their polling place had changed or that they were not properly registered to vote.[236]

On Election Day, a fake voter bulletin from the Franklin County Board of Elections was posted at polling locations, and fliers were distributed in the inner city, telling Republicans to vote on Tuesday and Democrats to vote on Wednesday due to unexpectedly heavy voter registration.[237]

In Cleveland, the *Washington Post* reported that unknown volunteers began showing up at voters' doors, illegally offering to collect and deliver complete absentee ballots to the election office.[238]

The Election Protection Coalition testified that, in Franklin County, voters received fliers informing them that they could cast a ballot on November 3.[239]

In Franklin County, there were reports that about a dozen voters were contacted by someone claiming to be from the County Board of Elections, telling them that their voting location had been changed.[240]

"Door-hangers" telling African American voters to go to the wrong precinct were distributed.[241]

ANALYSIS

The use of intimidation and misinformation in Ohio on Election Day was widespread and pervasive and clearly suppressed the vote. The NAACP testified that they received over 200 complaints of such acts in Ohio, so it is probable that the actual number of incidents ranged in the thousands. It is difficult to estimate how many of these incidents resulted in lost votes.

These incidents of voter intimidation and misinformation clearly violate the Voting Rights Act, the Civil Rights Act of 1968, Equal Protection, Due Process and the Ohio right to vote. The fact that Secretary Blackwell did not initiate a single investigation into these many serious allegations may represent a violation of his statutory duty to investigate election irregularities. Cases of intimidation and misinformation such as those we have seen in Ohio appear to have become a regular feature of our election landscape and would appear to warrant the development of a stronger investigative and law enforcement system than we have at present, at both the State and Federal levels.[242]

2. Machine Irregularities

FACTS

In the course of our hearings we learned:

In Auglaize County, there were voting machine errors. In a letter dated October 21, 2004, Ken Nuss, former Deputy Director of the County Board of Elections, claimed that Joe McGinnis, a former employee of ES&S, the company that provides the voting systems in Auglaize County, had access to and used the main computer that is used to create the ballot and compile election results. Mr. McGinnis's access to and use of the main computer was a violation of County Board of Elections protocol. After calling attention to this irregularity in the voting system, Mr. Nuss was suspended and then resigned.[243]

In Cuyahoga County and Franklin County, there were voting machine errors in connection with absentee ballots. The arrows on the absentee ballots did not align with the correct punch hole. This probably caused voters to cast a vote for a candidate other than the candidate they intended to support.[244]

In Mahoning County, one precinct in Youngstown recorded a negative 25 million votes.[245]

In Mercer County, one voting machine showed that 289 people cast punch card ballots, but only 51 votes were recorded for president. The county's website appeared to show a similar anomaly, reporting that 51,818 people cast ballots, but only 47,768 ballots were recorded in the presidential race, including 61 write-ins, meaning that approximately 4,000 votes, or nearly 7%, were not counted for a presidential candidate.[246]

At our Washington, D.C. hearing, investigative journalist Bob Fitrakis highlighted malfunctions in Lucas County: "When the machines in Lucas County, which is a heavily Democratic county, when they are locked in the principal's office and nobody may vote at that site; when they're going wrong all day, and the [Lucas County Election Director Paula Hicks-Hudson] admits the test failed prior to that, and the software is provided, of course, by Diebold, whose CEO, Walden O'Dell, is a member of President Bush's Pioneer and Ranger team, has visited the Crawford ranch and wrote a letter promising to deliver the electoral votes of Ohio—one has to be somewhat suspect [sic]."[247]

In Hamilton County, the *Washington Post* learned that many absentee ballots did not include Kerry's name because workers accidentally removed Kerry's name when they removed Ralph Nader's name from the ballots.[248]

ANALYSIS

There is no doubt that there were a number of machine irregularities and glitches in the election, beyond the major discrepancies highlighted earlier in our report. However, it is difficult for us to quantify the number of votes that were altered or affected by these irregularities.

Given the lack of cooperation we have received from the Secretary of State's office, it is difficult for us to ascertain whether the glitches were the result of mistake, negligence, or intentional misconduct. Depending on the type of misconduct involved, these errors may constitute violations of the Voting Rights Act, Equal Protection and Due Process, and Ohio's right to vote. Moreover, it would appear that Secretary Blackwell's apparent failure to follow up on these machine errors through an investigation, would be a violation of his duty to investigate election law irregularities.

The role of voting machines and computers in our election represents an increasingly serious issue in our democracy. Our concerns are exacerbated by the fact that there are very few companies who manufacture and operate voting machines, and they tend to be controlled by executives who donate largely, if not exclusively, to the Republican Party and Republican candidates. Issues such as the need for verifiable paper trails and greater accountability all warrant further investigation and possibly legislation.

3. Registration Irregularities and Official Misconduct and Errors

FACTS

In the course of our hearings we learned:

> A *Washington Post* investigation found that many longtime voters discovered their registrations had been purged.[249]

> Numerous voters were incorrectly listed on the roster as felons, and thus not allowed to vote.[250]

> The NAACP testified to receiving over 1,000 calls related to voter registration issues, generally from individuals who were not on the voter rolls, even though they had voted in previous elections; individuals with

questions on how to register, and individuals with concerns about not receiving a voter registration card.[251]

The Election Protection Coalition found that "[i]ndividuals frequently reported having 'disappeared' from the voter rolls . . . Many individuals expressed concerns that they had registered but never received confirmation or were not listed on the voter rolls at the precincts."[252]

At our Columbus, Ohio hearing, several documented problems in Cuyahoga County were brought to our attention by the Greater Cleveland Voter Registration Coalition (GCVRC).[253] GCVRC registered approximately 10,000 voters before the 2004 elections, yet when they tracked the registrations, 3.5% were either not entered at all or entered incorrectly, completely disenfranchising the applicants. [254] The Board of Cuyahoga County was alerted to this problem as early as September, but no corrective measures were taken.[255] Projected county-wide, over 10,000 people were probably not correctly registered and lost their right to vote.[256] These registration problems led to provisional ballots being thrown out.[257]

The NAACP reported that many voters complained that they were asked to show ID when they thought it was unnecessary, or were unable to vote because they lacked proper ID. At several locations in Cuyahoga County, all voters were being asked for ID, not just new voters. A voter called to say that all voters are being asked for ID, the poll workers were checking the address of the voter against the address on the registration and if they did not match, the voter was being turned away, often without casting a provisional ballot. In still another case, a voter was challenged because the address on the ID did not match the registration address, even though it was in the same precinct.[258]

There were numerous cases where election workers sent voters to the wrong precinct.[259]

A voter stated that a polling place in Cleveland ran out of ballots, and put in an emergency request for ballots, but did not receive them.[260]

The Associated Press reported that officials ticketed lawfully parked cars at the polling stations.[261]

Election Protection volunteers received complaints about provisional ballots from voters, many of whom reported being denied the opportunity to vote by provisional ballot. Some polling places either ran out of provisional ballots or never had any at their location. For example, when a voter, who had registered to vote in September, went to the polling place in Cuyahoga County on Election Day, the workers told her she was not registered and refused to give her a provisional ballot.[262]

In Franklin County, some voters who were standing in line waiting to vote outside the doors to the polling place, were sent home at 7:30 p.m. when the polls closed.[263]

ANALYSIS

Just as in the Florida presidential debacle four years ago, improper purging and other errors by election officials represent a very serious problem and have a particularly negative impact on Minority voters. The Greater Cleveland Voter Registration Coalition projects that in Cuyahoga County alone, over 10,000 Ohio citizens lost their right to vote as a result of official registration errors; and the NAACP received more than 1,000 purging complaints on election day—these facts indicate that the overall number of voters who may have been disenfranchised as a result of official mistakes and wrongful purging is in the scores of thousands, if not

more. Congressional passage of HAVA's provisional ballot requirement was intended to mitigate such errors, but Secretary Blackwell's unduly narrow interpretation of this requirement, as well as weak rules for counting and checking provisional ballots, have made it far less likely that individuals whose registration was wrongfully purged, or never entered, would be able to receive a provisional ballot and have it counted.

Given the information we have, it is unclear whether improper purging and other registration errors which appear so prevalent in Ohio, were the result of human mistake or intentional misconduct. **If it was intentional, a strong case can be made that it violated the Voting Rights Act, Equal Protection, Due Process, possibly the National Voter Registration Act, as well as Ohio's right to vote law. The Secretary of State's failure to investigate these registration errors and other irregularities may also violate his duties to do so under Ohio law.**

HAVA funds were supposed to be used to implement a fairer and more efficient registration system statewide. Unfortunately, full funding has been delayed, and most states, including Ohio, have received waivers from this Federal requirement.

C. GENERAL PROBLEMS

1. Spoiled Ballots—Hanging Chads Again?

FACTS

Ohio had a significant number of spoiled votes—approximately 93,000.[264] These are ballots in which either no Presidential vote was recorded or multiple votes were indicated and therefore ignored. For example, someone may not have filled in his presidential choice darkly enough for an optical scan machine to read, but did fill it in clearly enough to qualify as valid in a hand count.[265] Or a punch card voter may not have punched completely through his choice, leaving a "chad" attached that could not be read by the tabulator. But that same chad could be read in a hand count because Ohio law provides that hanging chads may be considered valid votes as long as two corners are detached.[266]

According to a *New York Times* investigation, "the problem [with spoiled ballots] was pronounced in minority areas, typically Kerry strongholds. In Cleveland ZIP codes where at least 85% of the population is black, precinct results show that one in 31 ballots registered no vote for president, more than twice the rate of largely white ZIP codes where one in 75 registered no vote for president. Election officials say that nearly 77,000 of the 96,000 [spoiled] ballots were punch cards."[267]

One of the principal purposes of the recount in Ohio was to ascertain the intent of these 93,000 ballots. However, by manipulation or otherwise, every county in Ohio except Coshocton County, avoided completing a full hand-recount. This means that the vast majority of these spoiled ballots will never be reviewed.

The problem was particularly acute in two precincts in Montgomery County which had an undervote rate of over 25% each—accounting for nearly 6,000 voters who stood in line to vote, but purportedly declined to vote for president.[268] This is in stark contrast to the 2% of undervoting county-wide.[269] Disturbingly, predominately Democratic precincts had 75% more undervotes than those that were predominately Republican.[270]

Secretary of State Blackwell has refused to answer any of the questions concerning these matters posed to him by

Ranking Member Conyers and eleven other Members of the Judiciary Committee on December 2, 2004.[271]

ANALYSIS

Given the high level of interest in the presidential election in 2004, it is logical to assume that many of the persons casting spoiled ballots intended to cast a vote for president, so this irregularity alone could account for tens of thousands of disenfranchised votes, with a disproportionate amount being Minority voters and Kerry voters. One of the reasons Ohio has such a large number of ballots is that the state relies so heavily on the outdated and antiquated punchcard system that proved to be error-prone in Florida. Sixty-eight of the eighty-eight Ohio counties still rely on the outdated punch card machines.[272] Thus, at least in the critical swing state of Ohio, the promise of HAVA funding to help states acquire better equipment so that more votes could count, has not been met.

With regard to the severe undercount voting figures in Montgomery County, we have not received any cooperation from Secretary Blackwell in ascertaining how this occurred. This may have been due to some equipment or poll worker error, or, in the worst case, manipulation.

2. Exit Polls Bolster Claims of Irregularities and Fraud

FACTS

An exit poll serves as a predictor of the final vote results in an election. It is conducted by interviewing voters about their vote selections as they are leaving the polls. The process for conducting reliable exit polls was largely created in 1967 by CBS News pollster and statistician Warren Mitofsky, who is considered "a world recognized expert in exit polling in particular and public opinion polling in general."[273] Former Mexican President Carlos Salinas credited Mr. Mitofsky's work for contributing to the prevention of fraud and an increase in credibility in the 1994 election in Mexico.[274]

The exit poll data taken on November 2, 2004, was compiled by two respected firms—Mitofsky International[275] and Edison Media Research. Joseph Lenski, who conducted the exit polls for Edison Media Research, trained in the field of exit polling under Mr. Mitofsky before starting his own firm.[276] Mitofsky and Edison conducted the 2004 exit polls under a contract from the National Election Pool (NEP), a consortium of six news and media organizations: the Associated Press, ABC, CNN, CBS, NBC, and Fox.

In this year's election, the National Election Pool conducted two types of exit polls: 73,000 voters were interviewed in statewide polls, and an additional 13,000 voters were interviewed for a national poll. The national poll's sample size was approximately six times larger than the sample normally used in high-quality pre-election national polls. This poll size would normally yield a very small margin of error and would be very accurate.[277] Furthermore, such a poll would normally result in a close congruence between exit poll and official results.[278] The sample size for Ohio was 1,963 voters, which is quite large for statistical purposes and equivalent to the 2,000-person norm for most national polls.[279] In addition, this year's poll numbers were designed to account for absentee votes because a large number of absentee votes contributed to the inaccurate projections of the Florida race in 2000. This year, Mitofsky and Edison began telephone surveys in key states before the election to screen for absentee voters and create an accurate estimate of their votes.[280]

While exit pollsters caution against using their results to predict election results,[281] exit polls can be extremely accurate, with only small variations from the official outcomes in numerous elections. For example, in the three most recent national elections in Germany, exit polls differed from the final official vote counts by an average of only 0.26%.[282] Their results have proven to be very accurate, correctly predicting the winner with no evidence of systematic skew of the data.[283] United States exit polls have also been precise. Brigham Young University students' exit poll results for Utah in this election indicated 70.8% for Bush and 26.5% for Kerry. The official results were 71.1% for Bush and 26.4% for Kerry.[284]

In the Ohio 2004 election, early exit polls, released just after noon on November 2, showed that Senator Kerry was leading President Bush by three percentage points.[285] Shortly after midnight on November 3, exit poll data continued to indicate that 52.1% of Ohio voters selected Senator Kerry and 47.9% selected President Bush.[286] These numbers, however, differed greatly from the final election results; in the official results, President Bush led Senator Kerry by 2.5 percentage points in Ohio.[287]

National poll data showed a similar shift from a clear advantage for Senator Kerry on Election Day to a victory for President Bush on the day after the election. Data that was provided by Edison/Mitofsky to the National Election Pool members at 4 p.m. on Election Day showed Senator Kerry leading 51% to 48%.[288] These percentages remained the same in the data released at 7:30 p.m. that day.[289] By the time Senator Kerry conceded the election on Wednesday, November 3, the Edison/Mitofsky poll numbers had been aligned with reported vote counts. For the first time, the poll numbers showed an advantage for President Bush with 51% to Senator Kerry's 48%.[290]

On December 3, 2004, Rep. Conyers requested the raw exit poll data from Mitofsky International.[291] Mr. Mitofsky replied, "The data are proprietary information gathered and held for the benefit of those news organizations, and I am not at liberty to release them."[292] On December 21, 2004, as a follow-up, Rep. Conyers requested the data directly from the newswire and television companies that contracted with Mr. Mitofsky and Mr. Edison for the data.[293] Though the Congressman has not received a response to his letter, Edie Emery, a spokesperson for the NEP and a CNN employee, said the exit poll data was still being analyzed and that the NEP's board would decide how to release a full report in early 2005.[294] "To release any information now would be incomplete," she said.[295] Furthermore, Jack Stokes, a spokesperson for the Associated Press said, "Like Congressman Conyers, we believe the American people deserve answers. We want exit polling information to be made public as soon as it is available, as we intended. At this time, the data is still being evaluated for a final report to the National Election Pool."[296]

ANALYSIS

Clearly something unusual is indicated by the differential between the exit poll information we have obtained and the final vote tallies in Ohio. It is rare, if not unprecedented, for election results to swing so dramatically from the exit poll predictions to the official results. Kerry was predicted to win Ohio by a differential of 4.2 percentage points. The official results showed Bush winning by 2.5 percentage points. The differential between the prediction for Kerry and the winning results for Bush represent a swing of 6.7 percentage points. According to University of Pennsylvania Professor Steven Freeman, this "exit poll discrepancy could not have been due to chance or random error."[297] **Professor Freeman has further concluded that statistical analysis shows a probability of 1 in 1,000 that the difference between Senator Kerry's share of the exit poll projection and the official count of the vote would be as much as the final 3.4% spread,[298] a virtual impossibility.**[299] As a matter of fact, there are broad statistical variations of up to nine percentage points between exit poll data and official results in Ohio and other key states in the 2004 election.[300] In state after state, Senator Kerry's advantage in the exit poll results was lost by sizable margins.

The discrepancy between the exit polls and the official vote count must be due to an inaccurate poll or an inaccurate vote. Either there was unintentional error in the exit poll or in the official vote count; either there was willful manipulation of the exit poll or of the official vote count— or other forms of fraud, manipulation or irregularities occurred in the electoral process. Pollsters Mitofsky and Lenski have indicated that their poll numbers deviated from the official results because a disproportionate number of Bush supporters refused to participate in their polls.[301] However, Professor Freeman posits that part of the discrepancy is due to a miscount of the vote.[302]

As noted above, election polls are generally accurate and reliable. Pollsters are able to categorize their sources of error and develop extensive methodologies to limit those errors with each successive poll.[303] Political scientist Ken Warren notes that ". . . exit polling has become very sophisticated and reliable, not only because pollsters have embraced sound survey research techniques, but because they have learned through experience to make valid critical adjustment."[304] In fact, prominent survey researchers, political scientists and journalists "concur that exit polls are by far the most reliable" polls.[305]

Unfortunately, throughout American history, various devices, schemes and legal structures have been used to shape election results. Elections at every level of government have been skewed by tactics that deny voting rights, establish poll taxes, lose voter registrations, disqualify voters and disqualify ballots to ensure a certain outcome. The 2000 Florida election provides ample evidence that our system is rife with election irregularites that profoundly impact our election outcomes.[306]

Elections are politically controlled, with extreme pressures for certain results. In our system, victory can become more important than an accurate vote count. While pollsters are privately hired based on their accuracy and timely reports, candidates and campaigns are primarily concerned with winning. When key election officials are also key campaign officials, as was the case in Florida in 2000 and in Ohio in 2004, the goal of providing an accurate vote tally falls into the murky waters of winning the political contest.[307] But pollsters lose their legitimacy and of course future contracts, if they are not accurate. Thus, "the systemic pressures on polling accuracy are much greater than they are on vote count accuracy."[308]

While pollsters use feedback and detailed analysis to improve their results, they are motivated to accuracy, and face market competition if they fail to provide thorough, accurate and timely exit poll results. "There is little competition, feedback and motivation for accuracy in election processing."[309] Thus we do not dismiss these exit poll results and their discrepancy with the official vote counts, as others might do. We believe they provide important evidence that something was amiss in the Ohio election.

Full, accurate and reliable statistical analysis cannot be completed until the raw data from the exit polls are released. The limited available "uncalibrated" or raw data indicates the broad discrepancies that are discussed above. However, it appears that the National Election Pool data was "calibrated" or corrected after the official results were publicized.[310] It may be standard practice to recalibrate poll results to reflect the actual outcome "on the assumption that the [official] count is correct, and that any discrepancies must have been due to imbalanced representation in their samples or some other polling error."[311] Thus, data that was publicized on Election Day showing these large discrepancies is no longer publicly available; only the recalibrated numbers are available on the Internet. An independent, detailed analysis of the early exit poll data is necessary to verify the actual outcome of the vote in Ohio, and to restore complete legitimacy to this election.[312] In any event, the discrepancies that we are able to identify place the entire Ohio election results under a cloud of uncertainty.

III. POST-ELECTION

A. CONFUSION IN COUNTING PROVISIONAL BALLOTS

FACTS

Secretary Blackwell's failure to issue standards for the counting of provisional ballots led to a chaotic and confusing result: each of Ohio's 88 counties could count legal ballots differently or not at all.[313] This inevitably led to the kind of arbitrary ruling which was made after the election in Cuyahoga County, where it was mandated that provisional ballots in yellow packets must be "rejected" if there is no "date of birth" on the packet. This ruling was issued despite the fact that the original "Provisional Verification Procedure" from Cuyahoga County stated, "Date of birth is not mandatory and should not reject a provisional ballot" and simply required that the voter's name, address and a signature match the signature in the county's database.[314] The People for the American Way Foundation sought a legal ruling ordering Secretary Blackwell and the County Elections Board to compare paper registration and electronic registration records.[315] People For the American Way further asked the Board to notify each voter whose ballot was invalidated about how the invalidation could be challenged.[316] Neither of these actions were taken.

In another case, while the counties were directed by the state to ensure that voters were registered during the thirty days before the election,[317] one college student who had been registered since 2000, and was living away from home, was denied a provisional ballot.[318]

ANALYSIS

Mr. Blackwell's failure to articulate clear and consistent standards for the counting of provisional ballots probably resulted in the loss of several thousand votes in Cuyahoga County alone, and the loss of untold more statewide. This is because the lack of guidance and the ultimate narrow and arbitrary review standards imposed in Cuyahoga County appear to have significantly contributed to the fact that in that county, 8,099 out of 24,472 provisional ballots, or approximately one third, were ruled invalid, the highest proportion in the state.[319] This number is twice as high as the percentage of provisional ballots rejected in 2000.[320]

These series of events constitute a possible violation of the Voting Rights Act, since the apparent discarding of legitimate votes undoubtedly had a disproportionate impact on Minority voters concentrated in urban areas like Cuyahoga County which had the highest shares of the state's provisional ballots. The actions may also violate Ohio's constitutional right to vote.

B. JUSTICE DELAYED IS JUSTICE DENIED—RECOUNTS WERE DELAYED BECAUSE OF A LATE DECLARATION OF RESULTS

FACTS

Ohio law requires the Secretary of State to provide County Boards of Elections with directives governing voting procedures, voting machine testing, and vote tallying.[321] Prior to the election, Secretary Blackwell thus issued a directive instructing Ohio Boards of Elections to complete their official canvasses by December 1,[322] almost one month after the date of the 2004 election. The directive further states that "no recount may be held prior to the official canvass and certification of results,"[323] so that County Boards would have to wait until Secretary Blackwell decided to certify the results before proceeding with recounts.

Ohio law also sets deadlines for the conduct of recounts. Firstly, applications for statewide recounts must be submitted within five days of the Secretary of State's declaration of results.[324] Secondly, such recounts must begin within ten days of the recount request.[325] Secretary of State Blackwell gave County Boards of Election until December 1 to certify their returns and then waited for another five days, until December 6, to certify the results. As a consequence, recounts could not be sought until at least December 11, and were required to begin by December 16. The Green/Libertarian recount began on December 13, 2004. As a result, the recount was pending when the Secretary of State sent certificates to electors on December 7, and before the Electoral College met on December 13. Because it appeared the Secretary of State had

intentionally delayed certification to ensure that the recount
could not be completed by these deadlines, eleven Members
of Congress, including Rep. Conyers, wrote to Gov. Taft asking that they delay or treat as provisional the December 13
meeting of the State's Presidential electors.[326]

The counties completed their recounts on December 28,
2004, but due to a variety of irregularities and alleged legal
violations in the recount, they remain embroiled in litiga-
tion as of the date of this report [Jan. 5, 2005].

ANALYSIS

The scenario created by Secretary Blackwell effectively pre-
cluded recounts from being concluded prior to the December
13 meeting of electors. By setting the vote tally deadline so late
and then delaying the declaration of results—it took a full thirty-
five days after the November 2 election for the results to be
certified—Secretary of State Blackwell ensured that the time
for completing recounts would not occur until after the date
of the Electoral College meeting.[327] It would appear that Mr.
Blackwell has intentionally ensured that the controversies concerning the appointment of electors could not be resolved by
December 7, 2004, thereby causing Ohio to lose the benefit of
the Electoral College "safe harbor" in which their appointment of electors is not necessarily binding on Congress. In
addition, this diminishment of the recount law may violate the
voters' right to Equal Protection and Due Process, as well as
undermine the entire import of Ohio's recount law.

C. TRIAD GSI—USING A "CHEAT SHEET" TO CHEAT THE
VOTERS IN HOCKING AND OTHER COUNTIES

FACTS

Perhaps the most disturbing irregularity that we have discovered in connection with the recount involves the activities

and operations of Triad GSI, a voting machine company. On December 13, 2004, House Judiciary Committee Democratic-staff met with Sherole Eaton, Deputy Director of Elections for Hocking County. She explained that on Friday, December 10, 2004, Michael Barbian, Jr., a representative of Triad GSI, unilaterally sought and obtained access to the voting machinery and records in Hocking County, Ohio.

Ms. Eaton saw Mr. Barbian modify the Hocking County computer vote tabulator before the announcement of the Ohio recount. Then, when the plan was announced that the Hocking County precinct was to be the subject of the initial Ohio test recount, Ms. Eaton saw Mr. Barbian make further alterations based on his knowledge of that plan. Ms. Eaton also has firsthand knowledge that Mr. Barbian told election officials how to manipulate voting machinery to ensure that a preliminary hand recount would match the machine count.[328] **A full state recount could be done only if the hand- and machine-recounts did not match, and it would appear that Mr. Barbian's manipulations were intended to insure that they did match.**

According to the affidavit, the Triad official sought access to the voting machinery based on the apparent pretext that he wanted to review some "legal questions"that Ohio voting officials might receive as part of the recount process. Several times during his interaction with Hocking County voting machines, Mr. Barbian telephoned Triad's offices to obtain programming information relating to the machinery and the precinct in question. It is now known that Triad officials have intervened in other counties in Ohio: Greene and Monroe, and perhaps others.

In fact, Mr. Barbian has admitted that he altered tabulating software in Hocking, Lorain, Muskingum, Clark, Harrison and Guernsey counties.[329] Todd Rapp, President of Triad, has also confirmed that these sorts of changes are standard procedure for his company.[330]

Firstly, during an interview, filmmaker Lynda Byrket asked Mr. Barbian, "You were just trying to help them so that they wouldn't have to do a full recount of the county, to try to avoid that?" Mr. Barbian answered, "Right." She went on to ask: "Did any of your counties have to do a full recount?" Mr. Barbian replied, "Not that I'm aware of."

Secondly, it appears that Mr. Barbian's activities were not the actions of a rogue computer programmer, but the official policy of Triad. Todd Rapp explained during a Hocking County Board of Elections meeting:

> The purpose was to train people on how to conduct their jobs and to help them identify problems when they conducted the recount. If they could not hand count the ballots correctly, they would know what they needed to look for in that hand count.[331]

Barbian noted that he had "provided [other counties] reports so they could review the information on their own."[332]

One observer asked, "Why do you feel it was necessary to point out to a team counting ballots the number of overvotes and undervotes, when the purpose of the team is to in fact locate those votes and judge them?"[333]

Barbian responded, ". . . it's just human error. The machine count is right . . . We're trying to give them as much information to help them out."[334]

In addition, Douglas W. Jones, a computer election expert from the University of Iowa, reviewed the Eaton Affidavit and concluded that it described behavior that was dangerous and unnecessary:

I have reviewed the Affidavit of Sherole L. Eaton ("the Eaton Affidavit"), the Deputy Director of the Hocking County Board of Elections, as well as the letter of Congressman John Conyers to Kevin Brock, Special Agent in Charge with the FBI in Cincinnati, Ohio. In light of this information, and given my expertise and research on voting technology issues and the integrity of ballot counting systems, it is my professional opinion that the incident in Hocking County, Ohio, threatens the overall integrity of the recount of the presidential election in Ohio, and threatens the ability of the presidential candidates, their witnesses, and the counter-plaintiffs in the above-captioned action, to properly analyze, inspect, and assess the ballots and the related voting data from the 2004 presidential election in Ohio. It is my understanding that 41 of Ohio's 88 counties use Triad voting machines. As a result, the incident in Hocking County could compromise the statewide recount, and undermine the public's trust in the credibility and accuracy of the recount.[335]

We have received several additional reports of machine irregularities involving several other counties serviced by Triad,[336] including a report that Triad was able to alter election software by remote access:

In Union County, the hard drive on the vote tabulation machine, a Triad machine, had failed after the election and had been replaced. The old hard drive was returned to the Union County Board of Elections in response to a subpoena.

The Directors of the Board of Elections in both Fulton and Henry County stated that the Triad company had reprogrammed the computer by remote dial-up to count only the presidential votes prior to the start of the recount.[337]

In Monroe County, the 3% hand count failed to match the machine count twice. Subsequent runs on that machine did not match each other nor the hand count. The Monroe County Board of Elections summoned a repairman from Triad to bring a new machine and the recount was suspended and reconvened for the following day. On the following day, a new machine was present at the Board of Elections office and the old machine was gone. The Board conducted a test-run followed by the 3% hand-counted ballots. The results matched this time, and the Board conducted the remainder of the recount by machine.

In Harrison County, a representative of the Triad company reprogrammed and retested the tabulator machine and software prior to the start of the recount. The Harrison County tabulating computer is connected to a second computer linked to the Secretary of State's Office in Columbus. The Triad technician handled all ballots during the machine recount and performed all tabulation functions. The Harrison County Board of Elections kept voted ballots and unused ballots in a room open to direct public access during daytime hours when the courthouse is open. The Board had placed voted ballots in unsealed transfer cases stored in an old wooden cabinet that, at one point, was said to be lockable and, at another point, was said to be unlockable.

On December 15, 2004, Rep. Conyers forwarded information concerning the irregularities alleged in the Eaton Affidavit to the FBI and to local prosecutors in Ohio.[338] He has not received a response to that letter. On December 22,

2004, Rep. Conyers forwarded a series of questions concerning this course of events to the President of Triad GSI and to Mr. Barbian.[339] Counsel for Triad GSI has indicated that a response would be forthcoming later this week or shortly thereafter. [This report was written toward the end of December or the first week in January.]

ANALYSIS

Based on the above, including actual admissions and statements by Triad employees, it strongly appears that Triad and its employees engaged in a course of behavior to provide "cheat sheets" to those counting the ballots. The cheat sheets told them how many votes they should find for each candidate, and how many over- and under-votes they should calculate to match the machine count. In that way, they could avoid doing a full county-wide hand recount mandated by state law. If true, this would frustrate the entire purpose of the recount law—designed randomly to ascertain if the vote-counting apparatus is operating fairly and effectively, and, if it is not, to conduct a full hand recount. By ensuring that election boards can conform their test recount results with the election-night results, Triad's actions may well have prevented scores of counties from conducting a full and fair recount in compliance with Equal Protection, Due Process, and the First Amendment.

In addition, the course of conduct outlined above would appear to violate numerous provisions of Federal and state law. As noted above, 42 U.S.C. §1973 provides for criminal penalties for any person who, in any election for Federal office, "knowingly and willfully deprives, defrauds, or attempts to defraud the residents of a State of a fair and impartially conducted election process, by . . . the procurement, casting, or tabulation of ballots that are known by the person to be materially false, fictitious, or fraudulent under the laws of the State in which the election is held." Section 1974 requires the retention and preservation of all voting records and papers for a period of twenty-two months from the date of a Federal election and makes it a felony for any person to "willfully steal, destroy, conceal, mutilate, or alter" any such record.[340]

Ohio law further prohibits election machinery from being serviced, modified, or altered in any way subsequent to an election, unless it is so done in the presence of the full Board of Elections and other observers. Any handling of ballots for a subsequent recount must be done in the presence of the entire Board and any qualified witnesses.[341] This would seem to operate as a *de facto* bar against altering voting machines by remote access. Containers in which ballots are kept may not be opened before all of the required participants are in attendance.[342] It is critical to note that the fact that these "ballots" were not papers in a box is of no consequence in the inquiry as to whether State and Federal laws were violated by Mr. Barbian's conduct: Ohio Revised Code defines a ballot as "the official election presentation of offices and candidates . . . **and the means by which votes are recorded.**" OHIO REV. CODE § 3506.01(B) (West 2004). Therefore, for purposes of Ohio law, electronic records stored in the Board's computer are to be considered "ballots." Triad's interference with the computers and their software would seem to violate these requirements.

Further, any modification of the election machinery may be done only after full notice to the Secretary of State. Ohio Code and related regulations require that after the State certifies a voting system, changes that affect "(a) the method of recording voter intent; (b) voter privacy; (c) retention of the vote; or (d) the communication of voting records,"[343] must be done only after full notice to the Secretary of State." We are not aware that any such notice was given to the Secretary.

Finally, Secretary Blackwell's own directive, coupled with Ohio Revised Code § 3505.32, prohibits any handling of these ballots without bipartisan witnesses present. That section of the code provides that during a period of official canvassing, all interaction with ballots must be "in the presence of all of the members of the board and any other persons who are entitled to witness the official canvass." The Ohio Secretary of State issued orders that election officials are to treat all election materials as if the State were in a period of canvassing,[344] and that, "teams of one Democrat and one Republican must be present with ballots at all times of processing."[345]

Triad has sought to respond to these charges by arguing that Ohio law requires a Board of Elections to prevent the counting or tabulation of other races during a recount and limit these activities to those offices or issues for which a formal recount request has been filed.[346] However, this requirement does not supersede the above requirements that election machinery only be serviced or otherwise altered in the presence of the full Elections Board and observers. There are at least two ways this recount process could have been conducted legally. Firstly, recounters could have been given the full ballot and been instructed simply not to count the other races recorded. Secondly, the service company employees could have waited to alter the software program until the official recount began in the presence of the Board and qualifying witnesses. Neither of these scenarios occurred in the present case.

In addition to these provisions imposing duties on the Board of Elections, there are numerous criminal penalties that can be incurred by those who actually tampered with the machines. These apply to persons who "tamper or attempt to tamper with . . . or otherwise change or injure in any manner any marking device, automatic tabulating equipment or any appurtenances or accessories thereof;"[347] "destroy any property used in the conduct of elections;"[348] "unlawfully destroy or attempt to destroy the ballots, or permit such ballots or a ballot box or pollbook used at an election to be destroyed; or destroy [or] falsify;"[349] and "willfully and with fraudulent intent make any mark or alteration on any ballot."[350]

It is noteworthy that Triad and its affiliates, the companies implicated in the misconduct outlined above, are the leading suppliers of voting machines involved in the counting of paper ballots and punch cards in the critical states of Ohio and Florida. **Triad is controlled by the Rapp family, and its founder Brett A. Rapp has been a consistent contributor to Republican causes.**[351] In addition, a Triad affiliate, Psephos Corporation, supplied the notorious butterfly ballot used in Palm Beach County, Florida, in the 2000 Presidential election.

D. GREENE COUNTY—LONG WAITS, THE UNLOCKED LOCKDOWN AND DISCARDED BALLOTS

FACTS

We have received information indicating negligence and potential tampering with Greene County ballots and voting machines. On December 9, election observers interviewed Carole Garman, the County Director of Elections, and found substantial discrepancies in the number of voting machines per voter in low-income areas as compared to other areas.[352] Apparently, some consolidated precincts had almost the state-imposed limit of 1,400 registered voters and others had only a few hundred voters.[353] One of the precincts disproportionately affected included Central State University and Wilberforce University, both historically black universities.[354]

The next day, the observers returned to that office and requested voter signature books for copying.[355] Ms. Garman granted such access.[356] After leaving the office for three hours, the observers returned and, having been advised that under Ohio law, they were entitled to copies of the precinct books for a nominal fee, they requested these copies from Ms. Garman.[357] Ms. Garman did not agree with that interpretation of Ohio law and telephoned the office of Secretary Blackwell, eventually reaching Pat Wolfe, the Election Administrator for the Secretary of State.[358] Ms. Garman then told the observers that, by order of Secretary Blackwell, all voter records for the State of Ohio were "locked down" and were now "not considered public records."[359] Ms. Garman subsequently physically removed the books from one observer's hands.[360] After attempting unsuccessfully to persuade Ms. Garman to reverse this decision, the observers left the office.[361]

The observers returned the following day, a Saturday, at 10:15 am.[362] While a number of cars were parked in the parking lot and the door to the office was unlocked, there was no one in the office.[363] One light was on that had not been on the previous night after the office was closed.[364] In the office, unsecured, were the poll books that had been taken from the observers the day before.[365] Also unsecured were voting booths, ballot boxes apparently containing votes, and voting equipment.[366] Shortly after the observers left the office, a police officer arrived and later elections officials came, along with members of the media.[367] The officials were unable to offer any explanation for the unsecured office, other than negligence; they said they would ask a technician (from the Triad company) to check out the machines on Monday.[368]

A number of other substantial irregularities in Greene County have come to our attention, uncovered after the office was discovered to be unsecured. In the short time that observers were allowed to examine voting records, ballots were not counted for apparently erroneous reasons.[369] In a number of cases, Greene County officials rejected ballots because the secrecy envelope for the ballot appeared to indicate that the voter had voted in the wrong precinct,[370] even though a notation had been made—apparently by an election worker—that the vote should count.[371] The records appeared to indicate that, in some cases, voters were sent to the wrong precinct by election workers and, in others, were given the wrong precinct's envelope for the ballot because election workers had run out of envelopes for the correct precinct.[372]

These records also seemed to show that some voters were purged from voting rolls because they had failed to vote in the previous election, while other voters who had not voted in several previous elections had not been purged.[373] On October 26, Secretary Blackwell issued a directive to Greene County officials regarding the "pre-challenging" process, in which a voter's eligibility is challenged prior to the election, and sent the Board of Elections an attached list of voters who were to be pre-challenged in Greene County.[374] Notice was sent by the Board to these voters by registered mail on the Friday before the election, advising such voters of their right to be present at a Monday hearing, where the voter's eligibility would be decided.[375] However, the notice probably did not arrive until the day of the hearing.

Other irregularities appear in the official ballot counting charts prepared by election officials, including many

264. Scott Hiaasen, "Like Clinging Chads, Kerry Faithful Hang On," *Cleveland Plain Dealer*, Nov. 6, 2004.

265. *Ibid.*

266. OHIO REV. CODE § 3515.04.

267. Dao et al., "Voting Problems."

268. Ken McCall & Jim Bebbington, "Two Precincts had High Undercounts, Analysis Shows," *Dayton Daily News*, Nov. 18, 2004.

269. *Ibid.*

270. *Ibid.*

271. Letter from John Conyers, Jr., Jerrold Nadler, Tammy Baldwin, Melvin L. Watt, Linda Sanchez, Robert Wexler, Maxine Waters, Sheila Jackson Lee, Martin Meehan, Zoe Lofgren, William D. Delahunt and Anthony Weiner to the Honorable J. Kenneth Blackwell, Ohio Secretary of State, Dec. 2, 2004. On file with the House Judiciary Committee Democratic Staff and at http://www.house.gov/judiciary_democrats/ohblackwellltr12204.pdf. Secretary Blackwell was asked to respond to the following:

> How many of those spoiled ballots were of the punch card or optical scan format and could therefore be examined in a recount?

> Of those votes that have a paper trail, how many votes for president were undercounted, or showed no preference for president? How many were over-counted, or selected more than one candidate for president? How many other ballots had an indeterminate preference?

> Of the total 93,000 spoiled ballots, how many were from predominately Democratic precincts? How many were from minority-majority precincts?

> Are you taking steps to ensure that there will be a paper trail for all votes before the 2006 elections so that spoiled ballots can be individually re-examined?

272. Dao et al., "Voting Problems."

273. *Moss v. Bush*, No. 04-2088 ¶ 66.

274. *Ibid. See also* Tim Golden, "Election Near, Mexicans Question the Questioners," *New York Times*, Aug. 10, 2004, at A3.

275. Mitofsky International's website states "Mitofsky International is a survey research company founded by Warren J. Mitofsky in 1993. Its primary business is conducting exit polls for major elections around the world. It does this work exclusively for news organizations. Mitofsky has directed exit polls and quick counts since 1967 for almost 3,000 electoral contests in the United States, Mexico, Russia and the Phillipines." http://www.mitofskyinternational.com/company.htm.

276. http://www.mitofskyinternational.com.

277. *Moss v. Bush*, No. 04-2088 ¶ 70.
278. *Ibid.*
279. Freeman at 10.
280. Howard Kurtz, "Networks Vow Caution in Calling Election; TV Executives Institute Reforms to Avoid Repeat of Erroneous 2000 Pronouncement," *Washington Post*, Oct. 12, 2004, at A7.
281. *Ibid. See also* David W. Moore, *The Superpollsters: How They Measure and Manipulate Public Opinion in America*, 258 (Four Walls Eight Windows 2d ed. 1995). "This caution in projecting winners is now a Mitofsky trademark, one which has served him well in most cases." Mr. Moore is Managing Editor of the Gallup Poll.
282. Freeman at 7.
283. *Ibid.*
284. Freeman at 8.
285. http://www.zogby.com/search/ReadClips.dbm?ID=10454.
286. Steven F. Freeman, "Who Really Won the 2004 US Presidential Election? An Examination of Uncorrected Exit Poll Data," Working Paper #04–10, Graduate Division, School of Arts & Sciences, Center for Organizational Dynamics, University of Pennsylvania, Nov. 12, 2004 (revised Nov. 23, 2004, additional grammatical changes Dec. 9, 2004), p.2, Based on calculations by author of "uncorrected" exit-poll data on CNN's website at 12:21 am Nov. 3, 2004 (http://www.cnn.com/ELECTION/2004/pages/results/ states/OH/P/00/epolls.0.htm), pp. 4–5.
287. http://serform.sos.state.oh.us/sos/boe/index.html.
288. United States General Exit Poll PRES04—Horizontal Percentages, filtered for all respondents, based on 8,349 interviews, weighted and created on 11/2/2004 at 3:59:05 PM.
289. United States General Exit Polls PRES04—Horizontal Percentages and PRES04—Vertical Percentages, both filtered for all respondents, based on 11,027 interviews, weighted and created on 11/2/2004 at 7:33:46 PM.
290. United States General Exit Polls PRES04—Horizontal Percentages and PRES04—Vertical Percentages, both filtered for all respondents, based on 13,660 interviews (just 2633 more interviews than were used in the 7:30 p.m. poll the night before), weighted and created on 11/3/2004 at 1:24:53 PM.
291. Letter from the Honorable John Conyers, Jr., Ranking Member, U.S. House Comm. On the Judiciary, to Warren Mitofsky, Mitofsky International (Dec. 3, 2004).
292. Letter from Warren Mitofsky to the Honorable John Conyers, Jr., Ranking Member, U.S. House Comm. on the Judiciary (Dec. 7, 2004).
293. Letters from the Honorable John Conyers, Jr., to Gail Berman, President, Entertainment, Fox Broadcasting Co., Anne Sweeny, President Disney-ABC Television Group; Jim Walton, President, CNN News Group; Bob Wright, Chairman and CEO., NBC; Thomas Curley, President, As-

sociated Press; and Andrew Heyward, President, CBS News; (Dec. 21, 2004).

294. "Michigan Congressman Seeks Poll Data," Associated Press, Dec. 22, 2004, available at http://news.bostonherald.com/politics and on the websites of many other Associated Press subscribers.

295. *Ibid.*

296. *Ibid.*

297. Freeman at 2.

298. *Moss v. Bush*, No. 04-2088 ¶ 73.

299. Freeman at 13.

300. Freeman at 2.

301. Steven F. Freeman, "Hypotheses for Explaining the Exit Poll-Official Count Discrepancy in the 2004 US Presidential Election" (DRAFT), provided by author, Jan. 3, 2004, p. 3.

302. *Ibid.*

303. *Ibid* at 7.

304. Mr. Mitofsky has worked on almost 3000 elections in his career and he has confirmed that the 2004 poll was conducted correctly. http://www.mitofskyinternational.com. Freeman, "Hypotheses" at 6.

305. Freeman, "Hypotheses" at 10.

306. Freeman, "Hypotheses" at 10–11 for discussion of lost, under-counted, over-counted and disqualified votes in that election.

307. The person empowered to determine the official vote count in Florida in 2000 was Florida Secretary of State Katherine Harris, who also served as co-chairwoman for the Bush/Cheney campaign in Florida that year. She was rewarded with strong GOP support for her successful Congressional campaign in 2002 and 2004. As noted, the current Ohio Secretary of State Ken Blackwell, who was equally empowered to determine the official Ohio vote, was also chairman of the Bush/Cheney campaign in Ohio for the 2004 election over which he presided.

308. Freeman, "Hypotheses" at 11.

309. Freeman, "Hypotheses" at 14.

310. *Moss v. Bush*, No. 04-2088 ¶¶ 25, 71. "The NEP 'corrected' its results by combining actual vote data with exit poll data to permit the exit poll results to conform to the reported 'official' results. In the process, any evidence of fraud as shown by a difference between the exit polls and the 'official' results was erased as the so-called exit poll results (as reported the day after the election on November 3, 2004) were forced to correspond to the 'official' results."

311. Freeman at 3.

312. Preserving Democracy—What Went Wrong in Ohio, Judiciary Democratic Forum (Dec. 8, 2004). Testimony of Shawnta Walcott, Communications Director, Zogby International at 84, "this election has produced unprecedented levels of suspicion regarding its outcome." *Ibid.* at 86, "We have received thousands of letters and phone calls regarding these

irregularities, many of which center on early exit polling results that were uncharacteristically inaccurate in several battleground states; questionable practices at polling stations that may have resulted in votes not being counted accurately, and in Ohio, as with other swing states, the automated Diebold machines were particularly disturbing."

313. Mark Niquette, "Lawsuits Focus on Provisional Ballots," *Columbus Dispatch*, Nov. 3, 2004, at 9A.

314. Bob Fitrakis, "And So the Sorting and Discarding of Kerry Votes Begins," *The Free Press*, Nov. 10, 2004.

315. *Ibid.*

316. *Ibid.*

317. *Ibid.*

318. Carl Chancellor, "Citizens Tell Panel of Voting Troubles," *Akron Beacon Journal*, Nov. 21, 2004, at B1.

319. James Ewinger, "Blackwell Sued Over Cuyahoga Vote Tally," *Cleveland Plain Dealer*, Nov. 27, 2004, at B3.

320. Diane Solov, "8,099 Cuyahoga Ballots Ruled Invalid," *Cleveland Plain Dealer*, Nov. 23, 2004.

321. OHIO REV. CODE §§ 3501.05(U), 3506.16.

322. Secretary of State J. Kenneth Blackwell, Directive No. 2004-43 (Oct. 25, 2004).

323. *Ibid.* at 4.

324. OHIO REV. CODE ANN. § 3515.02.

325. *Ibid.* § 3515.03.

326. Letter from the Honorable John Conyers, Jr. *et al.*, to the Honorable Bob Taft, Governor of Ohio, the Honorable Larry Householder, Ohio Speaker of the House, & the Honorable Doug White, Ohio Senate President (Dec. 13, 2004).

327. Anticipating the confluence of these deadlines, several plaintiffs, including two Presidential candidates, filed a lawsuit asking that Secretary Blackwell be ordered to ensure that recounts could be completed by December 7 (when Ohio had planned to certify its results for the Electoral College). *See, e.g., Rios v. Blackwell*, No. 3:04CV7724, 2004 WL 2668271, at *1 (N.D. Ohio). The Federal court denied their request on the grounds that the Presidential-candidate plaintiffs—Green Party candidate David Cobb and Libertarian Party candidate Michael Badnarik—were unlikely to win a recount. *Ibid.* at *2. It is unclear what the result of the lawsuit would have been had a viable Presidential candidate been a plaintiff.

328. Eaton affidavit on file with House Judiciary Committee Democratic Staff.

329. Preliminary Transcript, Interview of Michael Barbian by Lynda Byrket, on file with the House Judiciary Committee Democratic Staff.

330. Preliminary Transcript, Footage of Hocking County Board Meeting, Dec. 20, 2004, on file with the House Judiciary Committee Democratic Staff.

331. *Ibid.*
332. *Ibid.*
333. *Ibid.*
334. *Ibid.*
335. Affidavit of David W. Jones ¶ 12 (Dec. 15, 2004) (on file with House Judiciary Committee Democratic staff).
336. *Yost v. National Voting Rights Institute*, No. C2-04-1139 (S.D. Ohio) (decl. of Lynne Serpe).
337. Statement of Green Party County Coordinator, Henry County Recount, *available at* http://www.votecobb.org/recount/ohio_reports/counties/henry.php
338. Letter from the Honorable John Conyers, Jr., to Kevin R. Brook, FBI Special Agent in Charge, and Larry E. Beal, Hocking County Prosecutor (Dec. 15, 2004).
339. Letter from the Rep. John Conyers, Jr., to Brett A. Rapp, President, Triad GSI, and Michael Barbian, Jr., Ohio Field Rep, Triad GSI (Dec. 22, 2004).
340. Ohio law has a mirror provision which requires that all ballots be "carefully preserved" for 22 months.
341. OHIO REV. CODE § 3515.04.
342. *Ibid.*
343. OHIO ADMIN. CODE § 111:3-4-01 (2004).
344. Mehul Srivastava, "Greene County Elections Board Scrutinized; Office Containing Ballots Found Unlocked Overnight," *Dayton Daily News*, Dec. 12, 2004, at B1.
345. Secretary of State J. Kenneth Blackwell, Absentee/Provisional Counting and Ballot Security, Directive 2004-48 (Oct. 29, 2004).
346. OHIO REV. CODE § 3505.31.
347. *Ibid.* § 3599.27.
348. *Ibid.* § 3599.24.
349. *Ibid.* § 3599.34.
350. *Ibid.* § 3599.33.
351. Contributions of Brett A. Rapp:
    National Republican Congressional Committee:
    3/16/1998 $250
    2/15/1999 $350
    9/11/2000 $350
    Ohio State Central and Executive Committee:
    3/1/2001 $200
    Bush-Cheney 2004:
    2/2/2004 $500
    Republican National Committee:
    8/8/2003 $250
    2/3/2004 $500
    Source: http://www.fec.gov

352. Affidavit of Evelyn Roberson 1 (Dec. 12, 2004). Referring to observations on December 9, 2004. On file with the Democratic staff; Affidavit of Joan Quinn (Dec. 13, 2004). On file with the Democratic staff.
353. Roberson Aff.
354. Roberson Aff. *See also* Staff Interview with Katrina Sumner, January 3, 2005. The staff has also obtained information concerning the improper rejection of voter registrations of Central State University students that is currently under investigation.
355. *Ibid.*
356. *Ibid.*
357. *Ibid. Also see* Sumner Interview, January 3.
358. *Ibid.*
359. *Ibid.*
360. *Ibid.*
361. *Ibid.*
362. *Ibid.*
363. *Ibid.*
364. Sumner interview, January 3.
365. *Ibid.*
366. *Ibid.* While the ballot boxes were sealed and padlocked, they could be removed from the office.
367. *Ibid.*
368. *Ibid. See* discussion, *infra*, regarding Hocking County incident and Triad technician.
369. Staff Interview with Katrina Sumner, Green Party coordinator for the Greene County Recount, December 31, 2001.
370. *See* discussion, below, regarding Secretary Blackwell's bizarre legal dictates pre-and post-election, including new restrictions on provisional balloting, inconsistent with the law.
371. Staff Interview with Katrina Sumner.
372. *Ibid.* A notation by an election worker clearly indicates that "we donated green secrecy envelopes to another precinct to which they wrote their precinct number because they ran out of envelopes." (Emphasis added). A partial list of these voters is on file with staff. A number of voters are recorded as voting in precincts adjacent to the precinct in which they were registered.
373. *Ibid.*
374. Secretary of State J. Kenneth Blackwell, Directive 2004–44 (Oct. 26, 2004). On file with staff, including attachment.
375. Staff Interview with Katrina Sumner.
376. On file with staff.
377. Copies of ballot envelopes on file with staff.
378. OHIO REV. CODE § 3599.161.
379. *Ibid.*
380. *Ibid.*

381. *Ibid.* § 3505.31.
382. *Ibid.* § 3515.04.
383. *Ibid.* § 3599.16.
384. Secretary of State J. Kenneth Blackwell, Directive No. 2004-58 (Dec. 7, 2004).
385. *Yost v. National Voting Rights Institute*, No. C2-04-1139 (S.D. Ohio). Decl. of John C. Bonifaz.
386. Keith Cunningham, Director of the Allen County Board of Elections, characterized as frivolous any lawsuits attempting to force recounts, and considered mobilizing other Counties to oppose them. Terry Kinney, "Election Official Calls Recount Lawsuit Frivolous, Insulting," Associated Press, Nov. 22, 2004. One board, the Delaware County Board of Elections, sought and obtained a temporary restraining order preventing two Presidential candidates from forcing recounts. Mary Beth Lane, "Delaware County Court Blocks Recount," *Columbus Dispatch*, Nov. 24, 2004, at 7B. They took these positions even though the Ohio recount statutes do not provide any specific authorizations for counties to stop recounts from taking place.
387. *Yost v. National Voting Rights Institute*, No. C2-04-1139 (S.D. Ohio). Decl. of Lynne Serpe.
388. U.S. CONST. Amends. V, XIV.
389. *Bush v. Gore*, 531 U.S. 98, 104-05 (2000).
390. *Ibid.* at 98, 110.
391. OHIO REV. CODE ANN. § 3501.05(B)-(C).
392. Secretary of State J. Kenneth Blackwell, Directive No. 2004-58 5 (Dec. 7, 2004).
393. OHIO REV. CODE § 3515.03-04; Secretary of State J. Kenneth Blackwell, Directive No. 2004-58 5-6 (Dec. 7, 2004).
394. OHIO REV. CODE § 3515.04; Secretary of State J. Kenneth Blackwell, Directive No. 2004-58 5-6 (Dec. 7, 2004).
395. OHIO REV. CODE § 3515.03-04; Secretary of State J. Kenneth Blackwell, Directive No. 2004-58 3 (Dec. 7, 2004).
396. 377 U.S. 533, 555 (1964). *See also Yick Wo v. Hopkins*, 118 U.S. 356, 370 (1886). "The political franchise of voting" is a "fundamental political right, because preservative of all rights."
397. *Reynolds*, 377 U.S. at 554 (emphasis added; collecting cases); *Ibid.* "It is 'as equally unquestionable that the right to have one's vote counted is as open to protection . . . as the right to put a ballot in a box.'" Quoting *United States v. Mosley*, 238 U.S. 383, 386 (1915). "Obviously included within the right to choose, secured by the Constitution, is the right of qualified voters within a state to cast their ballots and **have them counted** . . ." *United States v. Classic*, 313 U.S. 299, 315 (1941) (Emphasis added).
398. *Reynolds*, 377 U.S. at 555; *Mosley*, 238 U.S. at 386; *Classic*, 313 U.S. at 315.
399. *Bush v. Gore*, 531 U.S. 98, 104 (2000).

400. *Mosley*, 238 U.S. at 386; *Griffin v. Burns*, 570 F.2d 1065 (1st Cir. 1978).
401. *Bonas v. Town of N. Smithfield*, 265 F.3d 69, 74 (1st Cir. 2001); *see also Marks v. Stinson*, 19 F.3d 873, 888 (3d Cir. 1994), finding that substantive due process violation exists where there is a "broad-gauged unfairness" that infects the results of an election; *Duncan v. Poythress*, 657 F.2d 691, 700 (5th Cir. 1981), holding that "the due process clause of the fourteenth amendment prohibits action by state officials which seriously undermine the fundamental fairness of the electoral process"; *Griffin v. Burns*, 570 F.2d 1065, 1077 (1st Cir. 1978), "If the election process itself reaches the point of patent and fundamental unfairness, a violation of the due process clause may be indicated and relief under § 1983 therefore in order"; *Siegel v. LePore*, 234 F.3d 1163, 1187 (11th Cir. 2000), a federally protected right is implicated "where the entire election process including—as part thereof the state's administrative and judicial corrective process—fails on its face to afford fundamental fairness". (Citations omitted).
402. Matter of Issue 27 on November 4, 1997, 693 N.E.2d 1190, 1193 (Ohio C.P. 1998).
403. *McKye v. State Election Bd. of State of Oklahoma*, 890 P.2d 954, 957 (Okla. 1995) (Emphasis added).
404. *Miller v. County Comm'n*, 539 S.E.2d 770, 776 (W. Va. 2000), "[I]nherent in the recount procedure is the concept of fairness to all interested candidates in an election. The recount procedure is the only mechanism available in an election dispute which gives the interested candidates a chance to identify and define problematic votes, thereby establishing the parameters for an election contest. . . . It is, therefore, evident that where the challenge to election results stems from specific votes cast, a recount plays an integral and indispensable role tantamount to fundamental principles of due process, which cannot be ignored or omitted."
405. Voting Rights Act of 1965 § 11, 42 U.S.C.A. § 1963i (2004) The Voting Rights Act was enacted in response to evidence that some States and Counties had denied many citizens access to the ballot because of their race, ethnicity, and language-minority status. Other major provisions of the act prohibit enactment of any election law that would deny or abridge voting rights based on race, color or membership in a language minority.
406. 42 U.S.C. § 1973gg *et seq*. This is the so-called "motor-voter" law.
407. *Ibid*. Specifically, the NVRA requires states to provide procedures so that eligible citizens may register to vote: (1) by application made simultaneously with an application for a motor vehicle driver's license; (2) by mail application; and (3) by application in person (A) at the appropriate registration site designated with respect to the residence of the applicant in accordance with state law; and (B) at a Federal, State, or nongovernmental office designated under Section 7 (required for State agencies

providing public assistance and agencies primarily engaged in providing
services to persons with disabilities).

408. In addition, a person who knowingly and willfully deprives, defrauds,
or attempts to deprive or defraud the residents of a State of a fair and
impartially conducted election process, by the procurement or submis-
sion of voter registration applications that are known by the person to
be materially false, fictitious, or fraudulent is guilty of a crime under
Section 1973gg-10 of Title 42. The act of engaging in fraudulent voter
registration practices, destroying voter registration forms, or otherwise
interfering with the ability of qualified voters to register, as prescribed
by law, are clearly covered by these statutes and demand prompt action
by the Department of Justice.
409. Pub. L. No. 107-252.
410. OHIO CONST. art. 5, § 1.
411. OHIO REV. CODE § 3505.10 (West 2004) (setting forth requirements
for a presidential ballot); *ibid.* §3 505.39 (describing the appointment of
electors and setting of meeting by the Secretary of State after the canvass); *ibid.* § 3505. 40 (requiring electors to vote for the candidate of the
political party they were slated to vote for).
412. *Ibid.* § 3501.05 (N)(1).
413. *Ibid.* § 3501.05 (W).
414. *Ibid.* § 3501.32.
415. *Ibid.* § 3501.35.
416. *Ibid.* §§ 3599.27, 3599.24, 3599.33-.34.
417. *Ibid.* § 3599.12.
418. *Ibid.* § 3505.24.
419. *Ibid.* §§ 3599.32, 3599.16-19.
420. *Ibid.* § 3505.35.
421. *Ibid.* § 3501.05(U).
422. *Ibid.* § 3515.04.
423. *Ibid.*
424. *Ibid.* § 3506.01(B).
425. OHIO ADMIN. CODE § 111:3-4-01 (2004).
426. Mehul Srivastava, "Greene County Elections Board Scrutinized; Office
Containing Ballots Found Unlocked Overnight," *Dayton Daily News*,
Dec. 12, 2004, at B1.
427. Secretary of State J. Kenneth Blackwell, Absentee/Provisional Counting
and Ballot Security, Directive No. 2004-48 (Oct. 29, 2004).
428. OHIO REV. CODE § 3599.27.
429. *Ibid.* § 3599.24.
430. *Ibid.* § 3599.34.
431. *Ibid.* § 3599.33.
432. *Ibid.* §§ 3515.01-.03.
433. *Ibid.* § 3515.05.

434. *Ibid.* § 3515.03.
435. *Ibid.*
436. *Ibid.* § 3515.04.
437. *Ibid.*
438. Secretary of State J. Kenneth Blackwell, Directive to All County Boards of Elections Directive No. 2004-58 (Dec. 7, 2004).
439. *Ibid.*
440. *Ibid.*
441. *Ibid.*
442. 3 U.S.C. §11.
443. U.S. CONST. Amend. XII.
444. 3 U.S.C. § 5.
445. "Congress shall be in session on the sixth day of January succeeding every meeting of the electors. The Senate and House of Representatives shall meet in the Hall of the House of Representatives at the hour of 1 o'clock in the afternoon on that day . . ." *Ibid.* §15.
446. *Ibid.* §18 ("no debate shall be allowed and no question shall be put by the presiding officer except to either House on a motion to withdraw.").
447. *Ibid.* §15.
448. *Ibid.*
449. *Ibid.*
450. *Ibid.*
451. *Ibid.* § 15.
452. In this latter case, the statute addresses three scenarios to dispose of duplicate slates of electors. First, only the votes from the electors properly appointed are counted. Second, when the slates are presented by two different State authorities who arguably have properly certified the electors, both Houses of Congress must concur as to which is the "lawful tribunal of such State" and accept the slate approved by that tribunal. And, finally, if there is no authority for which slate was lawfully appointed, both Houses of Congress must agree either to accept one set of electors over the other or to reject the electors from that state altogether.
453. In 1969 Senator Muskie and Representative O'Hara joined to file a objection against a "faithless elector" who cast a vote for George Wallace and Curtis LeMay instead of the candidate for whom he was expected to vote. The objection was debated and rejected by both houses. This is the only objection that has been raised since the 1887 Act in accordance with its requirements.